AMERICAN ARCHERY

A Vade Mecum of the Art of Shooting with the Long Bow

Compiled by
DR. ROBERT P. ELMER

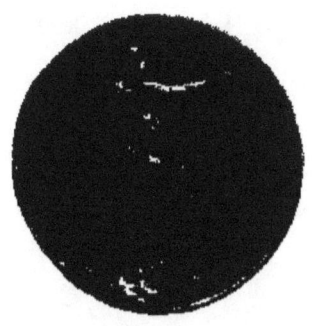

PUBLISHED UNDER THE AUSPICES OF THE
NATIONAL ARCHERY ASSOCIATION OF THE
UNITED STATES : : MCMXVII

PREFACE

This book was prepared as an act of the National Archery Association of the United States, and its publication authorized at the annual meeting of that body in 1916. It is made possible by the efforts of its principal author and its editor, both being Dr. Robert P. Elmer, present and for three years past Champion archer of the United States. American and other archers will be grateful to Dr. Elmer, not only for the filling of the great need for any current book at all on the sport, but for the excellence of his own contributions and for his diligence and discrimination in collecting the remainder of the chapters.

Two of the chapters are substantially of matter once published in *Forest and Stream*. Permission has been given for its reprinting herein. We are grateful

The format, the cover, the title page and other artistic requirements of the book have been made as they are by the advice and assistance of Mr. Arthur N. Hosking. We hope they are reasonably to his liking; and to him, also, we are grateful.

Preface

The medallion used on the cover and title page is from the medal designed by Mr. Cyrus E. Dallin. This beautiful work of art is pronounced by the Secretary of the American Numismatic Society to be the best medal ever produced in America. Frequent reference to awards of its replicas as prizes will be found in this book.

Acknowledgement is made of the work of the remaining authors.

The price of the book will be that necessary to support its publication. The wider currency it is given, the lower the price may be made for succeeding editions. If a profit is made, it will be the property of the National Archery Association of the United States. That profit will be expended for the furtherance of the sport. Therefore all promotion of the sale of this book and the making of gifts of it will work in a pleasing and profitable circle to the good of archery and archers. *Verbum sapienti.*

SAMUEL G. MCMEEN.

TABLE OF CONTENTS

Chapter	Author	Page
I.	History of American Archery. Dr. Robert P. Elmer	7
II.	Study of Correct Archery. Dr. Robert P. Elmer	21
III.	Equipment. Dr. Robert P. Elmer	33
IV.	Hints to Beginners. Samuel G. McMeen	40
V.	Constitution of the National Archery Association of the United States	47
VI.	How to Form an Archery Club. Dr. Robert P. Elmer	63
VII.	Highest Official American Scores. Dr. Edward B. Weston	67
VIII.	The Best English Scores. Dr. Edward B. Weston	69
IX.	Records of the National Archery Association of the United States. Dr. Edward B. Weston	73
X.	The Thirty-eighth Annual Tournament of the National Archery Association of the United States. James Duff	85
XI.	The Eastern Archery Association. Dr. Robert P. Elmer	103
XII.	Best Scores of All Kinds and Feats of Skill. Dr. Robert P. Elmer	114
XIII.	The Reddendo Arrows. J. Mark Mauser	152
XIV.	Scoring by "Points." Dr. Robert P. Elmer	156
XV.	Flight Shooting. Dr. Robert P. Elmer	160
XVI.	An American Origin for the Point of Aim. Dr. Robert P. Elmer	171
XVII.	Arrowhead, the Archers' Flower. Dr. Robert P. Elmer	176
XVIII.	French and Belgian Archery. Dr. Robert P. Elmer	178
XIX.	Choice of Woods for Bowmaking. James Duff	183
XX.	Bows and How to Make Them. J. M. Challiss	192
XXI.	Yew Bow Making. Dr. Harold G. Goldberg	220
XXII.	How to Make a Bowstring. L. W. Maxson	244
XXIII.	Notes on Arrow Making. Z. E. Jackson	247
XXIV.	The Composite Bow. Samuel G. McMeen	280
XXV.	Glossary. Dr. Robert P. Elmer	285

CHAPTER I

HISTORY OF AMERICAN ARCHERY
By Dr. Robert P. Elmer

IN THE minds of Americans the concepts relating to bows and arrows have two widely different derivations and yet, in the development of the sport of archery in this country, these sources are so intermingled that it cannot be said which has had the more potent influence. From prehistoric times to the present day the American Indians, though in constantly decreasing numbers, have used bows and arrows as their chief means of procuring food and as valuable weapons in war. Filled with tales of the frontier, boys without number have fashioned primitive imitations of the redman's equipment and have endeavored to emulate his prowess in the hunt and on the war-path. On the other hand the white man inherits legends of the bow from mediaeval Europe, with Robin Hood standing first in his imagination and behind him the archers of Crécy, Agincourt, the Wars of the Roses and the Norman Conquest, with hosts of others whom his reading of history and romance have furnished. More distant still are the classic bowmen of Greece and of the vanished empires of Africa and Asia.

These two streams of inspiration flowed together in the formation of the first archery club in America of which we have any record. "The United Bowmen of Philadelphia" was founded in 1828 by Titian Ramsey Peale. This young man, born in 1800, was a member of the famous family of artists of that name, and to secure drawings of the wild life of our West, he had accompanied, as assistant naturalist, the United States expedition under Major Long which explored the region from the Mississippi to the Rocky Mountains in 1819. From the Indians he had learned a love for the bow which he cherished until, a few years later, it led him to gather together five friends and start the club. To harmonize the sport with the conditions of civilization they were obliged to take as patterns the organizations already existing in England.

That "The United Bowmen" was prosperous is well proven. Its membership was limited to 25 and, in all the years of its existence a total of 57 had joined. They must have presented a brave appearance as they stood in line, for they shot from under a long pavilion which was supported by 25 poles, from each of which flew the flag of the archer beside it, and they were dressed in frock coats of Lincoln green, ornamented with gold braid, broad straw hats covered with green cloth and turned up with three black ostrich plumes, black belts and white pantaloons. The club published a little book called "The Archer's Manual," copies of which may still be found in public libraries. Its annual competitions were attended by as many as two thousand spectators, and not until 1858 did it stage its last contest.

In 1888 the surviving members met for the last time and deposited their trophies and archives with the Pennsylvania Historical Society, where they may now be seen. The trophies are in a showcase which can be opened only by breaking the glass. Chief among them is a superb punch bowl, awarded annually to the champion. His name was engraved on a tag suspended from the rim and he was expected to embellish the outside with a heavy, silver acanthus leaf. Other trophies are a silver goblet for the second man, a smaller goblet for the man who made the hit nearest the center and a brooch for the sixth man. Strangely enough the third, fourth and fifth men received nothing.

In 1859 the secretary wrote: "No grounds, no shooting." After that came the stirring events preceding the onset of the Civil War and archery suddenly ceased, to remain in desuetude for twenty years.

Its revival then was very similar to its origin, for again a young man hunted among the Indians and afterward introduced the sport to civilization. Maurice Thompson, a young Confederate veteran who, in the closing days of the war, had been wounded in the chest, returned to his home in Georgia only to find it in ruins. Ordered by his doctor to an open air life in a still warmer climate, and too reduced in circumstances to live by other than his own efforts, he and his brother Will H. Thompson journeyed to Florida and there encamped with an Indian guide. Fire-arms were forbidden them because of their recent belligerency, so they made crude bows and arrows. With practice they became excellent shots, game was superabundant, and as their skill in hunting increased they also learned to fashion better weapons.

Fortunately Maurice Thompson was "a writer as well as a fighter" and a few years later, in 1877 and 1878, he published a series of articles in Scribner's Magazine which related, in exquisite prose, his experiences in the woods and which, soon afterwards, were collected in a volume named "The Witchery of Archery." People at that time had no other lawn sport than croquet and they eagerly welcomed this more active exercise. Archery clubs sprang into existence as though by magic all over the United States, armed with anything from Indian weapons to the finest imported English goods.

The Chicago Archery Association conceived the idea of coördinating all this energy and so they issued a call for a convention of archery societies to meet at Crawfordsville, Indiana, where Maurice Thompson was then living, to consider the propriety of creating a National Archery Association for the United States of America. The meeting was held on January 23rd, 1879, in the office of the mayor, and was attended by representatives of clubs in eight cities. The organization was duly effected, with Maurice Thompson as president, and it was voted to hold the first Grand National Tournament at Chicago, for three days in August, 1879.

This tournament took place, as ordered, at White Stocking Park, now a part of Grant Park. Archers gathered from far and near, armed with material of every description, to the number of 89, a record of attendance which still remains unbroken. A brass band furnished music, caddies collected the arrows while the luxurious archers sipped refreshments, Society, in force, lent the glamor of its presence and about two thousand dollars worth of prizes, in cash, medals and merchandise, was competed for. Precedents were established of deciding the Championship by the Double York Round, the Woman's Championship by the Double Columbia Round, and the Men's Team Championship by the American Round. The names of the winners of the chief events in this and the succeeding tournaments can be found in the tables elsewhere. Of the participants the only one who are known to be still shooting are G. F. Henry and Tacitus Hussey, of Des Moines, Will H. Thompson, of Seattle, and Dr. E. B.

Weston, of Tropico, California, but until recently of Chicago. Homer S. Taylor, who is still one of the most skillful archers in the country, was present as a spectator.

The chief effect of this tournament was the general recognition of the N. A. A. as the center of influence in archery and of its annual tournament as the one preëminent archery event of the year.

The next two meetings were held in Buffalo and Brooklyn. They were both very successful but, after that time, interest in the game seemed to become centralized in Chicago, Washington and Cincinnati and the succeeding tournaments were held either in those cities or in places which might be considered as tributaries of them.

Changes in the program were made as experience widened. In 1881 the ladies began to shoot the Double National Round, as practiced in England, and thenceforward the championship was decided by that, instead of by the Double Columbia Round. Flight shooting was introduced in 1882 and, in the same year, the Team Contest was changed from a single American Round to its present form. The Team Contest for ladies was 72 arrows at 40 yards, in 1882 and 1883 and as at present, thereafter. In 1883 the Double American Round was invented, for the pleasure of those who did not care for the long range shooting, and the winner was recognized as the American Round Champion, although he was always acknowledged to be inferior in rank to the York Round Champion.

During the last decade of the nineteenth century the great popularity of tennis, cycling, and other fascinating sports did much to overshadow the lustre of archery, yet clubs continued to flourish, here and there, the annual tournaments were always held and the marksmanship of the contestants at them was almost uniformly meritorious. Until 1902 the chief stars were Maxson, Williams, W. A. Clark and W. H. Thompson among the men and Mrs. Howell and Mrs. Phillips among the ladies. The only records that survive from that period are the Flight Shot of 290 yards, by Maxson, the Single National of 68–398, by Mrs. Howell and the Double National of 132–756, also by her.

The year 1903 marks an epoch in archery in that it saw the return to the game of Dr. E. B. Weston, of Chicago. When it was decided that archery should have a place on the program of the Olympic Games, to be held in St. Louis in 1904, it was found that there was no one in the Middle West who was qualified to take the matter in charge. In this predicament Dr. Weston was persuaded to devote his energies to reviving the sport in that part of the country and he set about it with such vigor and persistence that his name is honored by every archer. After a rest of 19 years he shot at the tournament of 1903, at Niagara Falls, with amusing results. He himself delights in telling that out of 72 arrows at 100 yards he made 2–8, thus challenging the record of John Wilkinson who had made 1–9 in the previous year.

About this time, partly because of the Olympic Games, the spirit of vitality in archery became renascent and each succeeding year has seen it grow more robust. The 1904 tournament was held in the stadium at St. Louis and the shooting was done in a sea of mud. It had rained for fifteen hours before the contest began, so that it was necessary to furnish the archers with planks to stand on. At the end of the four days shooting some were still using them. During these two years the future champions Bryant and Richardson first appeared in competition.

In 1905 the tournament was held in Chicago, with the largest entrance list since 1889. Numerous archers of former days returned to the sport and new ones of great promise became interested.

In 1906 a successful meeting was held at Boston and then for five years the archers mustered at Chicago, mainly for the reason that Dr. Weston was willing to do all the hard work. While all these meetings were on a high plane, in every particular, that of 1910 is chiefly memorable, for there, shooting in a high wind, Harry B. Richardson made the American records of 116–566 for the Single York Round and 231–1111 for the Double York Round. In the Grand National of England this has been exceeded only once, in 1857, when Ford made the world's record of 245–1251.

At the end of this quinquennial it became apparent that the increasing number of archers in the East deserved recognition and so 1912 saw a highly successful tournament held at Boston, under the presidency of a new and enthusiastic archer, B. P. Gray. The range was laid out on the athletic field of Harvard University and luncheon was served in the adjacent stadium. The shooting was exceptionally good. G. P. Bryant made 230–1094 in the Double York Round, thus getting four figures for the second time in America, and he created the present records for the Single and Double American Rounds with 90–618 and 177–1153. For the first time three contestants got over 1000 in the Double American Round.

In 1913 Boston was the host again. The only noteworthy performance this year was Mrs. Bryant's record flight shot of 251 yards and 2/10 foot.

Since 1910 considerable interest in archery had been developing in some of the suburbs of Philadelphia, along the main line of the Pennsylvania Railroad, so it was voted to accept an invitation from the Merion Cricket Club at Haverford, to hold the 1914 tournament there.

The spacious house of this fashionable club offered every convenience to the archers and the velvet lawn, backed by stately trees, made a setting for the targets which has never been excelled in beauty. Although the entry list was unusually large, no important records were broken. The most interesting feature was the Double Columbia Round which was so closely contested that the relative position of the first three ladies depended on the last arrow.

Three successive tournaments in the East made it seem advisable to revisit Chicago in 1915. This meeting was handicapped by execrable weather. A wet chilling wind, such as is only too common in Chicago, swept in continually from the lake and on the last day there suddenly descended a deluge as though the flood gates of heaven had burst. In a few minutes the field was ankle deep with water, making it necessary to strike from the program all the events scheduled for that day. In spite of the bad conditions Miss Wesson made the records of 72–510 for the Single Columbia Round and 144–998 for the Double Columbia Round. She was shooting in such wonderful form that with better weather the national records would undoubtedly have been in serious danger.

In archery there is no line between professionals and amateurs, so the members of the N. A. A. were able to express their unanimous choice by electing James Duff, our popular fletcher, to be president for the following year, in which the tournament was held in his home town of Jersey City. The Scottish American Archers and the Clan McLeod took the big event under their canny guidance and the delightful result is fresh in the grateful memories of us all. Although the attendance was very satisfactory it would have been much larger had it not been for the apprehension produced by the great epidemic of infantile paralysis in the neighboring cities of Newark and New York. However, the shooting throughout was of a very high grade. For the second time three men passed the thousand mark in the Double American Round, for the third time the four figures were obtained in the Double York Round and the flight shot was within six inches of the record. The comfort of the archers was provided for in every way, particularly by a long awning for the ladies to stand under while shooting, a feature which recalled the pavilion of the United Bowmen of Philadelphia.

At the closing banquet about forty braw Scots appeared in full Highland costume, their bows and arrows replaced by dirk and skean-dhu. Here good-fellowship reigned supreme until the piper had squeezed the last tune through his chanter and the whole assembly, with arms crossed and hands clasped, had fervently sung "Auld Lang Syne."

CHAPTER II

STUDY OF CORRECT ARCHERY
By Dr. Robert P. Elmer

WHEN Roger Ascham, in 1542, wrote *Toxophilus*, "this Englishe matter in the Englishe tongue for Englishe men," he set the fashion for all future writers on archery by dividing the act of shooting with the long-bow into five parts, which he called, in the order of their occurrence, Standing, Nocking, Drawing, Holding and Loosing. As each of these is a step which must be mastered separately before the archer can rise to a plane of merit, I will still follow, in this short thesis, the "Scholemaster's" classic lead. At the same time I will try to present to the novice such other directions that he may know what to do from the moment he steps to the Shooting line till the arrow is quivered in its mark.

First of all he should study, with great care, the Constitution of the National Archery Association and, so far as possible, conform his shooting to its rules. After that, let us hope he may find what follows a guide to help him in practical shooting.

The six arrows, to be shot at one end, may be carried on the person, in a quiver or trouser's pocket, or they may be stood on the ground in front of the archer in some kind of receptacle.

To *string the bow*, grasp its handle with the left hand, the back of the bow being uppermost, and place the lower end, just above the tip, against the hollow of the left foot. Place the "heel" of the right hand against the upper end of the bow, below the loop of the string, and take the loop lightly between the thumb and forefinger. Then, holding the left hand steady, push hard with the right, letting it slide toward the nock and carrying the loop up till it falls into its groove. All pressure should be exerted on the bow, not on the string. To unstring the bow, bend it in the same way and pick the string out, lightly, with the first finger.

The correct *stand* is very important. In archery one does not toe the mark, he straddles it. The heels should be about nine inches apart in the line the arrow is to follow, the archer, therefore, standing with his left side toward the target. The feet may be either in their natural position or, as taught by Dr.

Study of Correct Archery 23

Weston, the left foot may be at right angles to the line of the heels and the right foot point about forty-five degrees backwards. The weight should be borne evenly by both feet.

The body should be perfectly erect.

The position of the head must vary somewhat with the individual. Classically, it should first be erect, as with a soldier at "Attention," and then turned sharply to the left so that the target is seen over the left shoulder. Yet for some people it is necessary to crane the neck, or tilt the head slightly, in order to provide for two essentials in archery, one, that the nock of the arrow be directly under the right eye, and the other that there be a clear way for the string. Many archers, especially ladies, find that in the orthodox position the string hits the left arm, elbow, shoulder or chest, causing great pain and ruining the shot. Such people must hold the shoulder well down and back and sometimes must even face slightly toward the target, changing the position of the feet accordingly.

To *nock* the arrow, grasp the bow-handle exactly as it will be held in shooting, the hand being even with the top of the handle, and hold the bow horizontal. Take the arrow by the nock, with the thumb and forefinger, and lay it on the bow, just touching the hand. Then fit it to the string, with the cock feather out, at exactly right angles, remembering that this relation is to the string and not to the bow, which may be crooked. During this operation the arrow may be steadied by the left fore finger, but it is not at all necessary to do so.

To *draw* the bow, hook the first three fingers under the string (the bow still being horizontal), with the arrow between the first and second, so that the string rests on the middle of the pads of the first joints. Then, turning the bow to a vertical position, raise the left arm stiffly, with elbow locked, straight away from the body, like a pump-handle, till the hand is level with the chin. Regarding the grip on the bow-handle there is a difference of opinion. Most authors say to grasp it with all one's strength but, personally, I prefer a very loose grip, the arm, and wrist however, being stiff as steel. The reason is derived from the fact, experimentally proven, that when a bow is held in a vise the arrow will fly far to the left. In shooting by hand an arrow goes straight because it pushes the bow a fraction of an inch to the right and, obviously, this can be done more freely when the grip is loose than when it is tight. After thus elevating the bow proceed, with such quick movements as to save one's strength for the aiming, to draw the string back so that the pile rests on the hand and the nock is directly under the right eye, not necessarily near that organ but somewhere, on the face or neck, in the vertical line dropped from it. At every shot, no matter what distance from the target, the arrow must be drawn to its full length and held there, until loosed, without being allowed to creep forward so much as an eighth of an inch. In drawing, keep the elbow free from the body and fully as high as the hand. This allows the powerful muscles of the shoulder and shoulder-blade to do most of the pulling and makes one feel that he "puts his body into the bow," as Bishop Hugh Latimer expressed it. The hand must follow in the line of the arrow, bending sharply from the forearm at the wrist.

The arrow must next be *aimed*, and the majority of archers do this with both eyes open. There are many, however, who close the left eye. It is probable that in target shooting one way is as good as the other, but in hunting it is quite necessary to use both eyes in order to judge distance. A beginner will often find, to his surprise, when his arrows are missing by wide margins, that he is not sighting with the right eye, as he thinks he is, but, inadvertently, is catching the aim with the left. In such a case he must shut the left eye until his vision be straightened out.

The most difficult thing in aiming and, indeed, in all archery, is the control of the nock end of the arrow. The tip can be seen, and its position accurately adjusted, but the rear end, which is just as important, must be controlled entirely by touch. Thus, some archers draw to the angle of the jaw, some to the corner of the mouth, some to a tooth (felt through the lip), some to the Adam's Apple and some to the end of the collar-bone but everyone, who wishes to shoot well, must find some part of his facial or cervical anatomy, in the line below the right eye, to which he can always draw the nock with unfailing precision.

The right hand being immovably fixed it follows that all variations in aim must be made by altering the position of the left hand, in either vertical or horizontal directions. This means that one must bear in mind two things, the line to the target, which is easily found by sighting along the shaft, and the elevation of the arrow. "Elevation" means the height of the tip with relation to the nock and is what determines the distance the shaft will fly. Forty-five degrees will give the greatest trajectory but much less is required for ordinary shooting. To get the correct elevation, and have it the same for each succeeding arrow, one must make use of an expedient originated by Horace Ford and called by him "The Point of Aim." The meaning of this term may be explained as follows.

When the arrow is fully drawn, and pointed in the line toward the target, the archer raises his left hand as much as his judgment directs and then, sighting over the tip of the pile, notes what his gaze falls on. Perhaps it is a dandelion, a lump of earth, a cloud or some other object. If, when shot from this elevation, the arrow hit the target, the object which the archer sees over his tip is his point of aim and he can get the correct trajectory for all his subsequent arrows by sighting their tips on that same point. If his arrow go too low, he must take a point of aim farther away, if too high, one nearer to himself. For most archers the point of aim at 100 yards is high in the sky and consequently impossible to find on certain shooting grounds. A special method of aiming, devised for this distance, is to paint a small white or black ring on the arrow, so placed that, when the elevation is right, the ring will be in line between the eye and the target. This is a good way but it requires considerable practice because, while the target is visible to the left eye, it is concealed from the right eye by the bow-hand. If, however, both eyes be kept open and the gaze centered fixedly on the target, there will be produced an optical illusion of looking *through* the bow-hand, with the ring on the arrow seen vaguely by indirect vision.

Authorities differ as to whether, in shooting at the shorter ranges, the gaze should be centered on the target, with the point of aim seen by indirect vision, or whether the latter should be in primary focus and the former seen only vaguely. Probably either way is correct, provided the archer be consistent and do not let his eye wander.

Holding is really a part of aiming. It refers to the time in which the arrow is held motionless just prior to the instant of flight, when that final coördination of eye and muscle is effected which is the acme of refined technique. Roger Ascham taught that this moment should be so brief as to be "better perceived in the mind than seen with the eye." Nevertheless, I have noticed that all the best shots in this country hold until they are perfectly certain that their aim is accurate and that all else is as it should be. In this connection I would say that a valuable, but difficult, thing to learn is to relax the string, without loosing the arrow, and begin the shot again when one feels that something is wrong. The frequent remark, "I knew that was not right before I shot it," is a reproach to the archer.

If the archer has nocked, drawn, aimed and held his arrow precisely as he has been directed to do he is now ready for the final act which frees the shaft from his control and leaves it to be guided only by the laws of physics. Of all things in the art of shooting *loosing* is the most important. Without a good loose all that has been done before counts for naught. I emphasize this particularly because most beginners seem to think that the aim is everything, forgetting that the flight of the arrow depends wholly on its position at the moment when it finally quits the string and on the propulsive force behind it, and that both of these factors may be ruined by the slightest side pull or sluggishness in loosing. To secure a good loose remember that the string must be borne on the first pad of each finger, and never hooked in the joint itself. Furthermore, the weight of the pull must be even on each finger. Usually the third finger has a tendency to carry most of the strain and the second much less, while the first finger takes up its share of the burden so reluctantly that it has been nicknamed, by Will Thompson, "The Shirking First."

The ideal loose is the one that liberates the string with a minimum of disturbance and retains the full tension of the bow up to the very last. It cannot be obtained by plucking the fingers off the string, as a harper twangs his instrument, because that would disconcert the aim. Neither will it suffice simply to open the fingers and let the string escape, for then the cast of the bow is lessened. The best way is to stiffen the arm still further, by a pull of the muscles that connect the shoulder-blade with the shoulder, as though one were continuing to draw, while the string is allowed to roll, at the same identical moment of time, off the tips of the three fingers.

It seems to me that Ascham should have added to his description of shooting a sixth division, which he might have called *pausing*, for, after the string has left the hand, the archer must stand, for a moment, like a statue, in the exact pose that he held at the instant of loosing. Otherwise he will find it impossible to keep the muscles at precisely the same tension while the arrow is crossing the bow. The left hand must not drop an iota and the right hand must remain resting firmly against the spot it has been drawn to. The best index at this point is the right elbow. If it has not dropped even a small fraction of an inch, the loose will probably have been a good one.

In conclusion I would say that in no sport is the need of exactness in detail greater than it is in archery and, also, that the practice which leads to virtuosity consists not so much in mere frequency of shooting as in the careful study of every shaft that is sped.

CHAPTER III
*Equipment
By Dr. Robert P. Elmer

THE beginner will find the following instructions helpful to him in selecting his equipment, or "Artillery" in the original meaning of the word.

Arrows

Of all things in the equipment of the archer the most important is the arrow. Unless every shaft be perfect and exactly like its fellows it is impossible to shoot well, no matter how good the rest of the tackle may be.

Arrows may be plain or footed. The former are made of one piece of wood and are fit only for toys. The latter have a shaft of soft wood with a "foot," or piece of hard wood, spliced on the pile end. This foot balances the arrow, so that it has a better

---

*Note.—It used to be that archery goods made in England were much better than those made in America. Of late years, however, our domestic products have been so much improved that now they fully equal, if they do not even surpass, the foreign makes.

flight, and also makes it much less liable to break. The shaft should be Douglas fir, spruce or Norway Pine. The foot may be of any strong, heavy wood.

The pile, or point, of the arrow should be in the shape of a cylinder with a bevelled end.

The nock, or slotted piece for the string, may be of fibre, horn or aluminum. The first two are wedge-shaped and set into the wood. The aluminum nocks are fitted over the end, like ferrules, and may be either tubular, as patented in England by Aldred, or cut from the solid bar, as used in America by Duff. Metal nocks are less apt to be injured when hit by another arrow, than are those of horn or fibre; the solid nocks are stronger than the tubular.

The best feathers are from the turkey. They should be stiff and cut to exactly the same shape. White, or brilliantly colored feathers, are better than those of sombre hues because they can be seen more readily in the grass.

Men's arrows should be 28 inches long, although a very tall or short man may require an inch more or less than that. They should weigh from 300 to 420 grains, in proportion to the strength of the bow. English arrows are marked in shillings; equivalent to 87¼ grains to the shilling.

Women's arrows should be 25 inches long and should weigh from 277 grains to 341 grains.

Bow

The parts of the bow are named as follows: Back, Belly, Upper Limb, Lower Limb, Handle and Nocks. Bows are of two kinds, self and backed. A self bow is made either of one long stave or of two short staves spliced at the handle. Backed bows are made of two or more strips of wood glued together, either continuous or spliced. By this means the back can be made of raw-hide, or more often, of some wood possessing great tensile strength, like hickory or the sap-wood of yew, while the belly is made of a soft wood capable of high resiliency under compression stress. Belgian and French bows, which are usually exquisitely made, often have three or even four laminae of wood but English and American bows seldom have more than the two.

Experts agree that the yew bow is the most pleasant to shoot, because of the smoothness of its draw. The relative merits of the self yew and yew-backed yew have been much discussed but the difference, if any exist, is practically negligible. In general it may be said that backed and self bows are equally good, the method of manufacture depending more on the material of which the bow is made than on anything else.

Although yew bows are nice to have they are very expensive and will not make a bit better scores than the cheaper lemonwood bows usually found in the shops. Bryant made the N. A. A. record for the American Round with a lemonwood bow and Rendtorff made his wonderful practice scores with one.

In selecting a bow, one should string it and see that the cord is then parallel to the handle. If this be not the case it means that one limb is too strong for the other. He should then pull the string back about a foot and let it go. If the bow give a big kick in the hand it shows that the two limbs do not return to their normal positions at the same moment. Next he should draw the full distance and note whether the curve of each limb be regular and whether the bow gives, or bends, in the hand. This latter is a grave fault, because the centre of the bow, for about eight inches, should not bend at all if the bow is to have a good cast.

Men's bows are six feet long and weigh from 35 to 55 pounds. By "weight," is meant the tractive force necessary to draw a 28 inch arrow to the head. Forty-two pounds is a good weight for the average man. The beginner almost invariably selects too strong a bow, not realizing that it is impossible to shoot accurately with strained muscles.

Women's bows are 5 feet 6 inches and weigh from 20 to 35 pounds for a 25 inch arrow.

Bracer

The bracer, or arm-guard, is a piece of leather laced to the flexor surface of the forearm to protect it from the whipping of the string. A very satisfactory kind is made of harness leather furnished with hooks like those on men's shoes.

Finger-Tips

The most popular protector for the fingers is made by reinforcing the tips of the first three fingers of an ordinary suede glove with pieces of thin, but stiff, leather.

Leather thimbles are preferred by some and are satisfactory if care be taken to get a perfect fit. The best kind has the end left open and the part over the finger nail cut away.

STRINGS

Before the war the best strings came from Germany and Belgium. At present it is necessary to use domestic strings, which are manufactured according to the directions given by Maxson elsewhere in this book.

QUIVER

Quivers are almost indispensable for women and are preferred by many men because of their cleanliness. All the patterns usually sold are satisfactory.

Many archers prefer to lay their arrows on a stool, or rack, in front of them, or to stand them in a vase. The heavy glass discs, perforated with several holes for holding separate flower stems, serve admirably. The holders made for surf-casting rods do very well.

Target Stands

These are simply made of three pieces of one inch by three inch white pine, with a loose bolt, or pintle, through them near the top. The outer staves are 6 feet long and the middle 6 feet 6 inches. They can be spread out to form a tripod to hang the target on. The string is simply thrown over the top, no special hook being necessary.

The iron stands sold by most dealers are pernicious in the extreme. They break the arrows almost constantly and should never be used.

Target

The target must be up to the full size of 4 feet in width and 4 inches in thickness. It should be well tested with the finger to see that the straw is thick and hard at every point, as a target that is soft, or loosely wrapped, is wholly useless.

The face should be painted in dull colors that will not glisten in the sun, and the red and blue rings should be in pale shades so that the arrows can be seen in them easily.

CHAPTER IV

HINTS TO BEGINNERS

By Samuel G. McMeen

THE best one hint to a beginner is: Follow the methods laid down by Dr. Elmer in the chapters in this book on correct archery and equipment.

There are a few points not touched upon by the authorities, however, on which one beginner perhaps may best be taught by another. It is probably for that reason that this chapter was assigned to the present writer.

One of these is the trouble of the arrow falling from the knuckle of the left hand as the latter is lifted to the shooting position and the draw is begun. The advice usually given to the novice on this point by the experienced archer is: "Keep on trying; that trouble will disappear in time. I used to be bothered by it years ago, but not for very long." Probably true, but not of much use to the beginner.

The writer's belief is that this falling of the arrow from the left hand is due to the failure of the first finger of the right hand to pull hard enough on the string, and to the consequent pressure of that forefinger downward on the arrow when the latter is in the horizontal position. That is, the string tends to pull the drawing fingers of the beginner into a full V with the nock of the arrow at the apex, while the fingers of the trained archer resist the string more fully and hold their portion of it more nearly vertical.

The remedy is to force the forefinger of the drawing hand to do its work. An expedient of help while that finger is getting trained, is to place the forefinger on the string a sensible distance from the arrow at the time of nocking, and so to prevent the pinching of the arrow that brings on the trouble of its sliding from the bow-hand knuckle. Make the forefinger do its work.

Another trouble of the beginner is that the side of the right forefinger next to the second finger develops soreness and perhaps a blister. To avoid this, consciously set that finger a little distance from the arrow at the time of nocking; use surgical tape on the tender part of the finger; if the will cannot control the muscles, fasten a bit of cork to the glove between those two fingers so that they *must* keep a little apart. Also, make the forefinger do its work.

Hold the breath during the acts of aiming and loosing.

Learn as early as you can what is meant by the "point of aim." It is not an abstruse subject. Some beginners practice it naturally from the outset. The whole subject may be said to be the art of hitting the target better by looking at something else than at the gold.

There is for an archer, with given equipment, only one distance at which on a calm day the point of the arrow will be directly between his right eye and the gold. That distance is more likely to be eighty yards than any other of the standard target distances. If it be eighty yards, and he shoot correctly in all other particulars, he can soon become a better archer at that distance than he is at a greater or less distance, *unless* he masters the point of aim. This he may do readily, if he will merely hold the point of the arrow between the right eye and some other object than the gold when shooting at distances other than the single one here assumed. At the greater distances, the point of aim of most archers is above the target. At all the distances of the American Round, the point of aim is on the ground in front of the target for all archers who draw to the bottom of the chin or below it.

Master the point of aim early in your career. See it by direct vision, and the gold by indirect. See that the arrow lies in the line to both the point of aim and the gold, unless wind-allowance is required. Keep the point of aim directly between you and the gold, unless wind-allowance is being made. If in doubt that you are standing in the right place to meet the last-named caution, hold your bow at arm's length so as to make a plumb-line of the string, and see if the latter cuts both the gold and the point of aim. You will be surprised at the untruths your eyes tell you. Check them up from time to time.

When a point of aim is established on a certain day and for a certain set of arrows and a certain bow and the certain state of your nerves and muscles, fix it firmly in mind by reference to surrounding objects so that it may not be lost or mistaken.

Have no shame in using an artificial object as a point of aim. Eggshells, gold balls, balls of paper, dandelions,—all legitimate. The ideal is a spherical mirror, smaller than a garden gazing-globe and larger than the bulb of a thermometer, as such an object reflects the image of the sun as a practical point, with no real area and with great but not blinding brilliance.

Make notes of your points of aim at the several standard distances. Carry a card with marks enabling you to take quick sights with the card at arm's length, instantly establishing the distance between the gold and the point of aim. Watch the first few arrows to see if the point is true under today's conditions.

Bows' strengths vary as the temperature rises and falls. Higher points of aim are necessary with the same bow on warmer days. Watch this.

To what exact point do you draw the nock end of the arrow? There have been champions who confessed they did not know, but they have no particular pride in that. The nock end of the arrow must be drawn to a point directly below the right eye, but that point may vary considerably in height. Find the one spot where the nature of your anatomy is best suited, and draw always to that spot.

Hints to Beginners

Decide for yourself, after full and careful trial, whether your form is best when gripping the bow-handle rigidly, or by the lower fingers of the left hand only, the upper part of the hand relaxed. When this is determined, follow the successful method to the complete exclusion of all others. Whatever the nature of the bow-hand grip, keep the left arm rigid at the instant of the loose.

Happy is the archer who has trained his left arm so as to make an arm-guard (bracer) unnecessary. Except for deformed anatomies, that training is possible. If the string touch anything but the nock of the arrow after leaving the fingers, that shot is impaired. Therefore: String your bow fully,—with due caution. Let the bracer, if you must use one, be of thin, firm, smooth leather. Watch its upper edge, that the string does not strike that.

Score your shooting and PRESERVE YOUR SCORES.

Not many archers can shoot without a glove or tips for the drawing hand. Make your own. A good way is to sew horsehide to the tips of the fingers of a kid glove. The kid need not be heavy. If the combination of the kid and horsehide is not thick enough, put parchment cut from the edge of your High School diploma between the kid and the horsehide. For the third finger, if it be tender, use a slip of quill instead of the parchment. Pare its edges. Slip in the quill or parchment after sewing all but the lower edge of the tip.

Use a round stick as a form inside the glove finger in sewing on the tips. Sew with fine silk thread, using several strands, waxed, taking close, small stitches. Let the horsehide cover three-fourths of the circumference of the glove finger.

CHAPTER V

Constitution of the National Archery Association of the United States

1. This organization shall be known as the National Archery Association of the United States of America.
2. The objects of the Association shall be to encourage the practice of archery and to arrange, each year, a Tournament to determine the archery championships of the United States.
3. The officers of the Association shall be a President, three Vice-presidents and a Secretary-Treasurer.
4. There shall be an Executive Committee, consisting of the five officers and four other members, of which the President shall be chairman. It shall have full control of the business and property of the Association, except when the Association is assembled in its Annual Business Meeting.
5. The officers, and the other members of the Executive Committee, shall assume

the functions of office within thirty days after their election and shall hold office until the qualification of their successors.

6. All records, fully completed, and the properly audited accounts, together with the funds and all other property of the Association, shall be turned over to the newly elected officers within thirty days after the close of the Annual Tournament.

7. A vacant office may be filled by a vote of a majority of the Executive Committee.

8. Anyone may be admitted to membership in the Association if recommended by a member in good standing and approved by the President and Secretary-Treasurer.

9. An application for membership must be accompanied by a Membership Fee of three dollars and an Annual Due of two dollars, which will be returned if the applicant be not accepted.

10. A member may be expelled by a vote of a majority of those present at an Annual Business Meeting.

11. Anyone may be elected to Life Membership, without dues, by a special vote at an Annual Business Meeting.
12. The Annual Due for each member shall be two dollars.
13. A member shall be suspended at the end of a fiscal year for non-payment of the dues of that year. He may be reinstated at any time by paying either his lapsed dues or the initiation fee, as he may prefer, together with the dues of the year in which his reinstatement occurs.
14. The fiscal year shall end at midnight of the last day of the Annual Tournament.
15. On being originally admitted to membership one shall pay a Membership Fee of three dollars.
16. The Association shall hold an Annual Tournament, between the 15th of July and the 15th of September, each Year. This Tournament shall be to determine the Archery championships of the United States and for such other forms of practice and competition in archery as are directed by the Executive Committee.
17. Before a member may participate in an Annual Tournament he must pay a

target fee of three dollars and must be free of all indebtedness to the Association, including the dues for the current year.

18. The Association shall hold an Annual Business Meeting during the Annual Tournament. At this meeting the officers and other members of the Executive Committee for the ensuing year shall be elected, the place for the next Annual Tournament decided upon and any other business transacted.
19. The Annual Tournament shall be under the supervision of the Executive Committee, which shall be represented by a Field-Captain. When possible the President shall be Field-Captain, but, if he cannot serve, the Executive Committee shall appoint one of the archers present.
20. The Field-Captain may appoint, to assist him, as many other general field officers as he may deem necessary.
21. At each target one archer shall be appointed by the Field-Captain to be Target Captain and another to be Scorer.
22. The following events for men must be shot at each Annual Tournament:

The Double York Round, consisting of
   144 arrows at 100 yards
    96   "   " 80   "
    48   "   " 60   "

The Double American Round, consisting of
   60 arrows at 60 yards
   60   "   " 50   "
   60   "   " 40   "

The Team Round for Men, consisting of 96 arrows at 60 yards.

The Flight Shoot for Men, consisting of 3 shots, not necessarily with different arrows.

23. The following events for women must be shot at each Annual Tournament:

The Double National Round, consisting of
   96 arrows at 60 yards
   48   "   " 50   "

The Double Columbia Round, consisting of
   48 arrows at 50 yards
   48   "   " 40   "
   48   "   " 30   "

The Team Round for Women, consisting of 96 arrows at 50 yards.

The Flight Shoot for Women, consisting of

    3 shots, not necessarily with different arrows.

24. Other events may be added at the discretion of the Executive Committee.
25. Any kind of bow, except a cross-bow, and any kind of arrow, may be used in any event.
25. The face of the target shall consist of a central disk, 9$\frac{3}{10}$ inches in diameter, and four concentric rings, each 4$\frac{3}{10}$ inches in width, painted, respectively, from within out, gold, red, blue, black and white.
27. The value of the colors shall be: Gold-9, Red-7, Blue-5, Black-3, White-1.
28. If an arrow cut two colors it shall count as having hit the inner one.
29. The targets shall be placed on easels, the center of the gold being four feet from the ground.
30. An arrow must remain in the target until recorded by the scorer.
31. An arrow rebounding from, or passing through, the scoring face of the target shall count as one hit and five in value.

32. Each archer shall shoot, at one time, six arrows, called an "end." Unless excused by his target captain he shall shoot three, yield place to his target mates and then, in his turn, shoot the other three.
33. The arrows of each archer must bear a distinctive mark.
34. Every arrow leaving the bow shall be deemed as having been shot if the archer, while standing within the line from which he has been shooting, cannot reach it with his bow. This rule is void if either the bow, string or arrow break during the shot.
35. A hit, or hits, made by an archer on a target not assigned to him shall not be counted.
36. All disputes shall be referred to the captain of the target at which they arise. From him an appeal may be taken to the Field-Captain, whose decision shall be final.
37. The Champion Archer of the United States shall be the archer who, in an Annual Tournament, has the highest result obtained by adding together the scores and hits of his Double York and

Double American Rounds. In case of a tie the archer with the greatest score wins. In case of a second tie the archer with the greatest score in the York Round wins.

38. Any woman, wishing to compete for the Championship of the United States or for the other titles competed for by the men, may shoot as a man, being subject to all the rules and conditions imposed on the men.

39. No man may compete in the events for women.

40. The Champion Woman Archer of the United States shall be the woman who, in an Annual Tournament, has the highest result obtained by adding together the scores and hits of her Double National and Double Columbia Rounds. In case of a tie the woman with the greatest score wins. In case of a second tie the woman with the greatest score in the Double National Round wins.

41. The word "Champion" shall be applied to none but these two.

42. The Winner of the Double York Round shall be the archer who has the highest

result obtained by adding together hits and score. In case of a tie the archer with the highest score wins. In case of a second tie the archer with the highest score at 100 yards wins.

43. The Winner of the Double American Round shall be the archer who has the highest score. In case of a tie the archer with the most hits wins. In case of a second tie the archer with the highest score at 60 yards wins.

44. No archer shall be allowed to shoot the first and second rounds of the Double American and Double York upon the same target.

45. The Winning Team of Men shall be the team of four archers, who must have been members of the same archery club for at least one month, which has the greatest aggregate score in the Team Contest. Three men may shoot as a team but their scores must count against those made by the four-men teams if any such compete. In case of a tie the team with the most hits wins. In case of a second tie the honors are divided.

46. The Winner of the Flight Shoot for Men shall be the man, or woman, who shoots an arrow the greatest distance. In case of a tie another arrow shall be shot.

47. The Winner of the Double National Round shall be the woman who has the highest result obtained by adding together hits and score. In case of a tie the woman with the highest score wins. In case of a second tie the woman with the highest score at 60 yards wins.

48. The Winner of the Double Columbia Round shall be the woman who has the highest score. In case of a tie the woman with the most hits wins. In case of a second tie the woman with the highest score at 50 yards wins.

49. The Winning Team of Women shall be the team of four women, who must have been members of the same archery club for at least one month, which has the greatest aggregate score in the Team Contest. Three women may shoot as a team but their scores must count against those made by the four-women teams if any such compete. In case of a tie the

Scoring

Photo. by Pearce

team with the most hits wins. In case of a second tie the honors are divided.

50. The Winner of the Flight Shoot for Women shall be the woman who shoots an arrow the greatest distance. In case of a tie another arrow shall be shot.

51. All prizes that are competed for at an Annual Tournament shall be awarded at an Annual Business Meeting or at an adjournment thereof. Those prizes that are the permanent property of the Association may be kept by their winners until 15 days before the next Annual Tournament, at which time they must be returned to the Secretary-Treasurer.

52. The Prizes for Men which are the permanent property of the Association shall be awarded as follows:
The York Medal to the Winner of the Double York Round.
The American Medal to the Winner of the Double American Round.
The 100 Yard Range Medal for the greatest score at 100 yards, barring the Champion and the Winners of the Double York and Double American Rounds.
The 80 Yard Range Medal for the great-

est score at 80 yards, barring the Champion, the Winners of the Double York and Double American Rounds and the Winner of the 100 Yard Range Medal.

The 60 Yard Range Medal for the greatest gross score at 60 yards in the Double York, the Double American and the Team Rounds, barring the Champion, the Winners of the Double York and Double American Rounds and the Winners of the medals for the longer ranges.

The 50 Yard Range Medal for the greatest score at 50 yards, barring the Champion, the Winners of the Double York and Double American Rounds and the Winners of the medals for the longer ranges.

The 40 Yard Range Medal for the greatest score at 40 yards, barring the Champion, the winners of the Double York and Double American Rounds and the Winners of the medals for the longer ranges.

The Maurice Thompson Medal for the greatest score at 100 yards.

The Spalding Medal for Men for the most Golds in the Double York Round.

The Potomac Medal for the greatest

score in the Team Round, whether the archer be a member of a team or not.

The Pearsall Bugle to the Winning Team of Men.

The Duff Arrow to the man, in his first National Tournament, who makes the greatest score in the Double American Round.

The Ovington Beaker to the Winner of the Flight Shoot.

The Jiles Cup to the man whose total obtained by adding together the hits and scores of his Double York and Double American Rounds shall show the greatest improvement over his similar total at the last National Tournament in which he took part. No scores more than 2 years old shall be counted.

The Clan McLeod Cup to the Winner of any Novelty Shoot that the Executive Committee may place on the program.

The Elmer Wooden Spoon to the man who, having shot through the whole of the Double York and Double American Rounds, shall have the lowest score in them.

53. The Prizes for Women which are the permanent property of the Association shall be awarded as follows:

The National Medal to the Winner of the Double National Round.

The Columbia Medal to the Winner of the Double Columbia Round.

The 60 Yard Range Medal for the greatest score at 60 yards, barring the Champion and the Winners of the Double National and Double Columbia Rounds.

The 50 Yard Range Medal for the greatest score at 50 yards in the Double National, Double Columbia and Team Rounds, barring the Champion, the Winners of the Double National and Double Columbia Rounds and the Winner of the 60 yard Range Medal.

The 40 Yard Range Medal for the greatest score at 40 yards, barring the Champion, the Winners of the Double National and Double Columbia Rounds and the Winners of the medals for the longer ranges.

The 30 Yard Range Medal for the greatest score at 30 yards, barring the Champion, the Winners of the Double National and Double Columbia Rounds and the Winners of the medals for the longer ranges.

The Spalding Medal for Women for the most Golds in the Double National Round.

The Peacock Cup to the Winning Team of Women.

The Maid Marian Arrow to the Archer, in her first National Tournament, who makes the greatest score in the Double Columbia Round.

The Sidway Medal to the Winner of the Flight Shoot.

The Jessop Trophy to the Winner of the Wand Shoot.

The C. C. Beach Junior Brooch to the girl under 18 who makes the greatest score in the Double Columbia Round. If no archer fulfills these requirements it shall be awarded to the youngest woman present, no matter what her score may be.

54. The Dallin Medal in Gold shall be given outright to the two Champions but to no one else.
55. The Dallin Medal in Silver or Bronze may be given outright to the Winners

of such conditions or events as may have been announced by the Executive Committee before the beginning of the Tournament.

56. *Special Prizes may be awarded at the discretion of the Executive Committee.
56. All previous constitutions are hereby revoked.
57. This constitution may be altered or amended only at an Annual Business Meeting of the Association, and by a two-thirds majority of those present.

*NOTE.—The only special prize now in possession of the Association (June, 1917) is the Weston Trophy, which is not numbered among the permanent prizes because it becomes the property of the archer who wins it three times in succession. It is awarded as follows: The Weston Trophy shall be awarded to the archer, of either sex, who makes the most Golds at any one end of six arrows during the Tournament. All claims must be accompanied by a record of string measurement from the pin-center to the inner edge of each arrow.

CHAPTER VI

How to Form an Archery Club

By Dr. Robert P. Elmer

THOSE veteran archers who are supposed to be authorities on toxophilitic subjects are continually asked the question, "How can one form an archery club?" Taking their experience as a guide, the answer to this simple query may be outlined as follows.

The person who wishes to start the club is usually one who, for some reason or other, has become an enthusiastic archer. In course of time he tires of shooting alone and plans to create an organization, both for the pleasure of companionship and to promote his beloved sport.

How shall he secure active members for it? This is the one great problem. Archery is a sport in which it is so difficult to become proficient that, of those who essay a beginning only a small proportion persist until they acquire enough skill to make shooting a real pleasure.

It is well, therefore, for him to interest as many beginners as he can and, to do this, no way is so effective as to fit them out and let them shoot with equipment loaned for the occasion. Some are sure to be fascinated sufficiently to wish to continue and, with a nucleus of three or four such neophytes, a club may safely be started.

After thus securing the archers a permanent range must be found. It may be on the grounds of a country club, on the lawn of a member or in any available field. Of course the more agreeable the surroundings the easier it is to lengthen the roll of members. Preferably the range should be at least 120 yards long, so that the York Round may be shot, but, in many cases, it is not possible to get more than the 80 yards required for the American and National Rounds. Nearby there should be a place where targets can be stored.

Not more than two officers are necessary, a President, who acts *ex officio* as Field Captain, and a Secretary-Treasurer.

The actual shooting should follow the rules laid down in the Constitution of the National Archery Association, except that in small

How to Form an Archery Club 65

matches several archers usually toe the line simultaneously and use all six arrows at once, instead of three, in order to save time.

Dues should be sufficient to provide for the purchase of new targets each year, and to pay for keeping up the range. Small entrance fees for stated matches and tournaments will furnish money for prizes.

To maintain interest there is nothing better than the holding of frequent matches between the individuals of the club and, when possible, with teams from other clubs. The contests for individuals may be scratch events when the archers are fairly equal in skill but, as a general rule, more fun can be had by handicapping each one according to his ability. Various methods of arranging handicaps are in use. Some clubs take as a basis the last score, some strike an average of three or more recent performances and some handicap on the best mark the archer has ever made. In the last case most of the cards handed in will be minus, but the incentive to do one's best is constant and there is no chance for an individual to win merely because he has had a recent slump.

Of course, as in any other undertaking, many problems of a local nature will arise which must be decided by one's own judgment but, if the founder of the club will be guided by these hints and, more particularly, by the Constitution of the National Archery Association he will probably be able to start a successful and permanent organization.

CHAPTER VII

HIGHEST OFFICIAL AMERICAN RECORDS

Made in Annual Tournaments of the National Archery Association

By Dr. Edward B. Weston

	Hits-Score	Place	Date
Single York Round			
H. B. Richardson	116– 566	Chicago	1910
Double York Round			
H. B. Richardson	231–1111	Chicago	1910
Single American Round			
G. P. Bryant	90– 618	Boston	1912
Double American Round			
G. P. Bryant	177–1153	Boston	1912
Men's Team Round			
Individual			
G. P. Bryant	92– 556	Boston	1912
Team of 4 Men			
Chicago Archery Association,		Chicago	1907
A. E. Spink	87– 461		
H. S. Taylor	89– 417		
W. H. Thompson	89– 413		
C. C. Beach	85– 389		
	250–1680		
Flight Shoot, Men			
L. W. Maxson	290 yards	Natural Bridge, Va.	1891
Single National Round			
Mrs. M. C. Howell	68– 398	Dayton	1895
Double National Round			
Mrs. M. C. Howell	132– 756	Dayton	1895

Single Columbia Round
  Miss C. M. Wesson   72– 510   Chicago   1915
Double Columbia Round
  Miss Cynthia M. Wesson   144– 998   Chicago   1915
Women's Team Round
  Individual
    Mrs. M. C. Howell   91– 507   Dayton   1893
  Team of 4 Women
    Wayne Archers
      Miss Wesson   94– 482
      Mrs. Trout   86– 412
      Mrs. Dunlap   68– 330
      Mrs. Elmer   47– 181
                                      295–1405   Haverford   1914
Flight Shoot, Women
  Mrs. G. P. Bryant   251 yards $\tfrac{4}{10}$ foot   Boston   1913

CHAPTER VIII

THE BEST ENGLISH SCORES

By Dr. Edward B. Weston

SINCE the beginning of the five public meetings in England, in 1853, there have been made only 17 double York round scores of over 1000, two of them being over 1100 and one over 1200. These three high scores were made by Ford, the only archer who has made in public a higher score than our Henry B. Richardson who, in 1910, scored 231–1111. The complete list follows:

Grand National

1854	H. A. Ford	234–1074
1857	H. A. Ford	245–1251 (World's Record)
1858	H. A. Ford	214–1076
1867	H. A. Ford	215–1037

Leamington

1856	H. A. Ford	244–1162
1857	H. A. Ford	230–1026
1858	H. A. Ford	230–1128
1861	H. A. Ford	212–1014
1868	H. A. Ford	219–1087
1869	H. A. Ford	220–1030

Great Western

1870	C. H. Fisher	225–1033
1872	C. H. Fisher	218–1060
1886	C. E. Nesham	202–1022

Southern Counties

1905	J. B. Keysworth	216–1016

Crystal Palace

1882	H. H. Palairet	221–1025
1893	F. A. Govett	214–1004
1901	C. E. Nesham	217–1027

From 1883 to the present time the championship score at the Grand National has been as high as 900 only five times, Mr. C. E. Nesham making four of the scores, one of which, for 1886, is given above, and Mr. Fisher making the other.

As is indicated by the above records, Mr. Ford was by far the best archer produced by England within historically authentic times. His private scores are far ahead of those made in the great public meetings and, up to the present time, have not been approached dangerously near by anyone.

His best single York round was shot with a yew-backed yew and 5s., 29 inch arrows.

	66–344	47–301	24–164	137–809
Second best;	69–371	48–274	24–154	141–799

Although he does not specifically mention the weight of the bows used in these rounds it is elsewhere stated by him that he usually shot a 56 pound bow.

His best double York round, shot privately, (Butt's "Ford," p. 281), was:

61–295	48–306	24–186	133– 787
63–299	46–278	24–168	133– 745
			266–1532

According to Butt, the best marks he ever made at the three ranges are included in the above scores, namely:

		Gold	Red	Blue	Black	White
At 100 yards	69–371	12	17	19	14	7
" 80 "	48–306	10	19	15	2	2
" 60 "	24–186	10	13	1		
	141–863					

After reading these wonderful scores it may possibly be a comfort to young archers to learn that Mr. Ford's first appearance at the Grand National he made a double York round of 101–341.

Other English archers who have made over 600 at the single York round are:

Capt. A. P. Moore	133–691	Private practice.
John Bramhall	125–675	25th November, 1851.
G. E. S. Fryer	127–639	Practice at Royal Toxophilite Society.
C. E. Nesham	128–632	Private practice at Bournemouth. 14 May, 1883.
E. A. Holmes	134–622	Private practice at Harrow. 1867.
C. J. Perry-Keene	126–604	Private practice. 24 July, 1886.

In shooting the double national round many ladies have passed the 700 mark; but few have made 800, as shown on the following page:

Grand National

Year	Archer	Score
1892	Miss Legh	140–804
1894	Mrs. C. Bowley	133–823
1898	Miss Legh	143–825
1902	Miss Legh	137–813
1903	Miss Legh	142–802
1904	Miss Legh	143–841
1905	Miss Legh	141–807
1907	Miss Legh	143–809
1911	Miss Q. Newall	141–803

Grand Western

Year	Archer	Score
1881	Miss Legh	144–840
1910	Miss Wadsworth	139–807

Leamington

Year	Archer	Score
1885	Mrs. Piers F. Legh	142–864
1888	Miss Legh	141–817
1895	Miss Legh (World's Record)	142–866
1900	Miss B. M. Legh	138–824
1903	Miss Legh	140–800
1906	Miss Legh	141–803
1907	Miss Q. Newall	133–801
1908	Miss Legh	138–808

(The Leghs were three different ladies.)

Crystal Palace

Year	Archer	Score
1885	Miss Legh	143–809
1890	Miss Legh	142–862
1893	Mrs. C. Bowley	140–822

It would seem that, in comparing the skill of the past and present great archers, Miss Legh should be ranked the equal of Mr. Ford.

CHAPTER IX

RECORDS OF THE NATIONAL ARCHERY ASSOCIATION OF THE UNITED STATES

By Dr. Edward B. Weston

DOUBLE YORK ROUND

		100 yards	80 yards	60 yards	Total
1879	W. H. Thompson	70-236	63-233	39-155	172-624
1880	L. L. Peddinghaus	55-221	56-274	41-211	152-708
1881	F. H. Walworth	67-261	64-262	42-240	173-763
1882	H. S. Taylor	55-151	67-275	46-252	168-678 (a)
1883	R. Williams, Jr.	76-300	79-371	44-236	199-907
1884	W. H. Thompson	63-237	68-314	43-209	174-760
1885	R. Williams, Jr.	91-357	78-360	46-278	215-995
1886	W. A. Clark	43-195	72-298	43-225	158-718
1887	W. A. Clark	42-134	64-244	43-201	149-579
1888	W. H. Thompson	66-244	71-309	38-180	175-733 (b)
1889	L. W. Maxson	66-220	68-308	46-238	180-766
1890	L. W. Maxson	62-252	59-231	45-235	166-718
1891	L. W. Maxson	53-197	66-304	44-218	163-719
1892	L. W. Maxson	58-216	72-310	42-196	172-722
1893	L. W. Maxson	59-241	60-220	45-253	164-714
1894	L. W. Maxson	58-202	57-213	38-184	153-599
1895	W. R. Robinson	61-283	67-241	41-225	169-749
1896	D. F. McGowan	43-161	38-132	37-159	118-462
1897	W. A. Clark	59-221	59-223	41-189	159-633
1898	L. W. Maxson	61-241	63-259	35-277	159-677
1899	M. C. Howell	51-185	53-215	34-170	138-590
1900	A. R. Clark	59-213	76-342	45-205	180-758
1901	W. H. Thompson	61-237	57-229	45-215	163-681

(a) Mr. Taylor won by points, Mr. D. A. Nash making 167 hits, 713 score.
(b) Mr. Thompson won by points, Mr. Maxson making 171 hits, 739 score.

		100 yards	80 yards	60 yards	Total
1902	R. Williams, Jr.	56-212	56-228	38-172	150-612
1903	W. Bryant	50-212	66-240	41-201	157-653
1904	G. P. Bryant	79-281	67-293	46-246	192-820
1905	G. P. Bryant	72-274	59-259	41-183	172-716
1906	H. B. Richardson	81-331	79-367	41-193	201-891
1907	H. B. Richardson	73-307	66-312	45-241	184-860
1908	W. H. Thompson	88-362	78-368	45-243	211-973
1909	G. P. Bryant	102-402	80-330	45-243	227-975
1910	H. B. Richardson	96-400	89-445	46-265	231-1111
1911	H. S. Taylor	78-338	63-259	40-228	181-835
1912	G. P. Bryant	105-435	78-374	47-285	230-1094
1913	Dr. J. W. Doughty	66-282	66-254	46-266	178-802 (c)
1914	Dr. R. P. Elmer	58-238	58-270	46-256	162-764
1915	H. L. Walker	49-183	60-262	43-221	152-666
1916	Dr. R. P. Elmer	90-390	74-364	46-266	210-1020

(c) Dr. Doughty won by points, Mr. G. P. Bryant making 176 hits, 832 sco re

DOUBLE AMERICAN ROUND

		60 yards	50 yards	40 yards	Total
1883	Col. R. Williams, Jr.	56-290	60-392	60-404	176-1086
1884	Col. R. Williams, Jr.	57-301	50-356	59-367	176-1024
1885	Col. R. Williams, Jr.	57-295	60-356	60-404	177-1055
1886	W. A. Clark	59-213	60-388	60-396	179-1097
1887	W. A. Clark	54-266	60-342	60-384	174- 992
1888	L. W. Maxson	59-277	56-280	60-404	175- 961
1889	J. T. Shawan	52-256	59-315	60-380	171- 951
1890	L. W. Maxson	51-255	59-341	60-400	170- 996
1891	L. W. Maxson	54-244	60-362	60-402	174-1008
1892	L. W. Maxson	57-287	60-354	60-400	177-1041
1893	L. W. Maxson	60-324	57-323	58-336	175- 983
1894	J. Benckenstein	50-240	60-292	59-339	169- 871
1895	L. W. Maxson	53-287	59-325	60-402	172-1014
1896	L. W. Maxson	54-272	56-306	60-364	170- 942
1897	W. A. Clark	48-208	54-284	57-299	159- 791
1898	J. L. Taylor	50-246	57-315	58-324	165- 885
1899	W. A. Clark	46-234	57-265	56-312	159- 811

Photo. by Paul Thompson

MISS CYNTHIA M. WESSON
Champion Woman Archer of the United States, 1915, 1916, 1917
(No tournament held in 1917)

National Association Records

		60 yards	50 yards	40 yards	Total
1900	A. R. Clark	58-312	60-338	59-375	177-1025
1901	C. S. Woodruff	51-275	48-248	60-330	159- 853
1902	Col. R. Williams, Jr.	50-286	55-283	59-361	164- 930
1903	Col. R. Williams, Jr.	53-251	58-298	59-345	170- 878
1904	G. P. Bryant	56-270	60-366	60-412	176-1048
1905	C. C. Beach	56-280	58-354	60-372	174-1006
1906	H. B. Richardson	59-331	59-341	60-380	178-1052
1907	Col. R. Williams, Jr.	56-296	59-333	60-380	175-1009
1908	Col. R. Williams, Jr.	52-282	58-336	59-389	169-1007
1909	G. P. Bryant	56-322	60-380	60-416	176-1118
1910	H. B. Richardson	59-291	58-362	60-406	177-1059
1911	Dr. R. P. Elmer	56-362	59-361	60-418	175-1041
1912	G. P. Bryant	58-338	59-373	60-442	177-1153
1913	Dr. R. P. Elmer	54-248	57-329	59-423	170-1000
1914	Dr. R. P. Elmer	56-312	60-332	60-408	176-1052
1915	Dr. R. P. Elmer	57-299	60-364	60-412	177-1075
1916	Dr. R. P. Elmer	54-306	59-359	60-400	173-1065

Rank of the Winners of the Double York Round

		Times Winner	Av. Winning Scores	Highest Score	Av. All Scores	No. Contests
1.	Richardson	3	207- 955	231-1111	164- 704	8
2.	G. P. Bryant	4	205- 901	230-1094	188- 828	7
3.	Elmer	2	186- 892	210-1020	171- 761	6
4.	Williams	3	188- 838	215- 995	166- 716	14
5.	Doughty	1	178- 802	178- 802	178- 802	1
6.	Walworth	1	173- 763	173- 763	159- 677	2
7.	A. R. Clark	1	180- 758	180- 758	164- 702	2
8.	H. S. Taylor	2	179- 757	181- 835	163- 691	14
9.	Thompson	5	178- 754	211- 973	162- 680	18
10.	Robinson	1	169- 749	169- 749	155- 629	2
11.	Peddinghaus	1	152- 708	152- 708	123- 537	2
12.	Maxson	7	166- 702	180- 766	136- 564	17
13.	Walker	1	152- 666	152- 666		
14.	W. A. Clark	3	155- 643	158- 718	125- 507	15
15.	Howell	1	138- 590	138- 590	118- 492	10
16.	McGowan	1	118- 462	146- 544	106- 410	10

Rank of the Winners of the Double American Round

		Times Winner	Av. Winning Scores	Highest Score	Av. All Scores	No. Contests
1.	G. P. Bryant	3	176–1102	177–1153	169– 991	7
2.	Richardson	2	177–1055	177–1059	178– 846	8
3.	Elmer	5	174–1046	177–1075	174–1050	6
4.	A. R. Clark	1	177–1025	177–1025	164– 622	4
5.	Williams	6	174–1008	176–1086	169– 919	11
6.	Beach	1	174–1006	174–1006	163– 886	11
7.	Maxson	7	174– 992	177–1041	161– 855	19
8.	Shawan	1	171– 951	171– 951	162– 862	4
9.	W. A. Clark	4	168– 898	179–1097	159– 827	23
10.	J. L. Taylor	1	165– 885	165– 885	151– 749	7
11.	Benckenstein	1	169– 871	169– 871	139– 657	8
12.	Woodruff	1	159– 853	171– 933	160– 820	6

Champions

Men

1879–1914	The Winner of the Double York Round.
1915	Dr. R. P. Elmer Score 2012
1916	Dr. R. P. Elmer Score 2468

Women

1879–1880	The Winner of the Double Columbia Round.
1881–1914	The Winner of the Double National Round.
1915	Miss C. M. Wesson Score 1980
1916	Miss C. M. Wesson Score 1692

TEAM CONTEST FOR MEN
(4 a side)

American Round

1879	Wabash Merry Bowmen, Crawfordsville, Ind.	302–1508
1880	Marietta Archers, Marietta, Ohio	314–1640
1881	College Hills Archery Club, Cincinnati, Ohio	315–1611

Team Round

1882	College Hills Archery Club, Cincinnati, Ohio	309–1435
1883	Highland Archery Club, Wyoming, Ohio	294–1332
1884	Battle Creek Archery Club, Battle Creek, Mich.	315–1428

Photo by Paul Thompson

Dr. ROBERT P. ELMER
Champion Archer of the United States, 1914, 1915, 1916, 1917
(No tournament held in 1917)

TEAM ROUND—Continued.

Year	Team	Score
1885	Highland Archery Club, Wyoming, Ohio	327–1509
1886	Highland Archery Club, Wyoming, Ohio	285–1283
1887	Brooklyn Archery Club, Brooklyn, N. Y.	301–1349
1888	Highland Archery Club, Wyoming, Ohio	316–1636
1889	Walnut Hills Archery Club, Cincinnati, Ohio	291–1367
1890	Walnut Hills Archery Club, Cincinnati, Ohio	314–1486
1891	Walnut Hills Archery Club, Cincinnati, Ohio	283–1307
1892	Walnut Hills Archery Club, Cincinnati, Ohio	311–1367
1893	Walnut Hills Archery Club, Cincinnati, Ohio	297–1383
1894	Potomac Archers, Washington, D. C. No other team present.	
1895	Walnut Hills Archery Club, Cincinnati, Ohio	286–1294
1896	Potomac Archers, Washington, D. C.	252–1086
1897	Potomac Archers, Washington, D. C.	297–1335
1898	Highland Archery Club, Wyoming, Ohio	284–1314
1899	Highland Archery Club, Wyoming, Ohio	275–1181
1900	Highland Archery Club, Wyoming, Ohio	306–1334
1901	Potomac Archers, Washington, D. C.	296–1314
1902	Potomac Archers, Washington, D. C.	287–1343
1903	Potomac Archers, Washington, D. C.	284–1242
1904	Potomac Archers, Washington, D. C.	300–1334
1905	Chicago Archery Club	309–1367
1906	Boston Archers	327–1591
1907	Chicago Archery Club	350–1680
1908	Chicago Archery Club	318–1532
1909	Boston Archers	300–1436
1910	Chicago Archery Club	330–1506
1911	Chicago Archery Club	318–1528
1912	Boston Archers	324–1618
1913	Boston Archers	328–1538
1914	Wayne Archers, Wayne, Pa.	320–1578
1915	Stopped by rain at the end of the first half, with the Wayne Archers in the lead	
1916	Keystone Archers	342–1582

FLIGHT SHOOT FOR MEN

		Yards	Inches
1882	J. Wilkinson, Chicago	213	
1883	No contest		
1884	No contest		
1885	W. P. Webb, Eaton, Ohio	234	
1886	J. J. Watrous, Cincinnati, Ohio	210	
1887	L. W. Maxson, Washington, D. C.	226	
1888	L. W. Maxson, Washington, D. C.	233	
1889	L. W. Maxson, Washington, D. C.	266	
1890	L. W. Maxson, Washington, D. C.	268	18
1891	L. W. Maxson, Washington, D. C.	290	
1892	L. W. Maxson, Washington, D. C.	213	
1893	C. J. Strong, Cincinnati, Ohio	285	18
1894	L. W. Maxson, Washington, D. C.	253	
1895	G. Benckenstein, Wyoming, Ohio	247	
1896	L. W. Maxson, Washington, D. C.	250	
1897	L. W. Maxson, Washington, D. C.	240	
1898	L. W. Maxson, Washington, D. C.	247	
1899	L. W. Maxson, Washington, D. C.	224	
1900	L. W. Maxson, Washington, D. C.	251	
1901	R. E. Taylor, Cincinnati, Ohio	230	
1902	A. E. Whitman, Melrose, Mass.	244	
1903	L. W. Maxson, Washington, D. C.	246	
1904	L. W. Maxson, Washington, D. C.	259	
1905	W. Bryant, Boston	241	
1906	H. S. Taylor, Chicago	230	
1907	H. B. Richardson, Boston	218	
1908	J. M. Challis, Atchison, Kan.	232	
1909	Z. E. Jackson, Atchison, Kan.	245	
1910	H. W. Bishop, Chicago	213	8
1911	Dr. R. P. Elmer, Wayne, Pa.	270	9
1912	G. P. Bryant, Boston	229	24
1913	Dr. R. P. Elmer, Wayne, Pa.	260	12
1914	J. S. Jiles, Pittsburgh	234	¼
1915	No contest, on account of rain		
1916	G. P. Bryant, Boston	289	28

DOUBLE NATIONAL ROUND

		60 yards	50 yards	Total
1881	Mrs. A. H. Gibbs	61-233	36-160	97-393
1882	Mrs. A. H. Gibbs	63-251	38-198	101-449
1883	Mrs. M. C. Howell	85-413	47-277	132-690
1884	Mrs. H. Hall	46-204	42-212	88-416
1885	Mrs. M. C. Howell	75-353	46-252	121-605
1886	Mrs. M. C. Howell	82-386	44-238	126-624
1887	Mrs. A. M. Phillips	83-385	48-246	131-631
1888	Mrs. A. M. Phillips	82-424	42-258	124-682
1889	Mrs. A. M. Phillips	89-481	44-232	133-713
1890	Mrs. M. C. Howell	79-353	46-226	125-579
1891	Mrs. M. C. Howell	59-221	45-243	104-464
1892	Mrs. M. C. Howell	79-353	48-272	127-625
1893	Mrs. M. C. Howell	84-380	45-247	129-627
1894	Mrs. A. Kern	67-343	45-237	112-580
1895	Mrs. M. C. Howell	86-474	46-282	132-756
1896	Mrs. M. C. Howell	81-361	45-249	126-610
1897	Mrs. J. S. Barker	70-294	42-226	112-520
1898	Mrs. M. C. Howell	88-428	44-210	130-638
1899	Mrs. M. C. Howell	84-426	46-242	130-668
1900	Mrs. M. C. Howell	81-387	44-268	125-665
1901	Mrs. M. C. Howell	34-146	33-145	67-291
1902	Mrs. C. S. Woodruff	82-366	44-238	126-604
1903	Mrs. M. C. Howell	87-381	48-272	135-653
1904	Mrs. M. C. Howell	87-417	43-203	130-620
1905	Mrs. M. C. Howell	80-366	44-204	124-570
1906	Miss E. C. Cooke	48-180	34-122	82-302
1907	Mrs. M. C. Howell	78-386	45-233	123-619
1908	Miss H. A. Case	60-248	32-150	92-398
1909	Miss H. A. Case	79-343	46-234	125-577
1910	Miss J. V. Sullivan	71-399	44-230	115-629
1911	Mrs. J. H. Taylor	53-197	41-199	94-396
1912	Mrs. J. H. Taylor	66-304	46-220	112-524
1913	Mrs. P. S. Fletcher	63-271	30-106	93-377
1914	Mrs. B. P. Gray	81-387	46-238	127-625
1915	Miss C. M. Wesson	85-455	45-253	130-708
1916	Miss C. M. Wesson	80-356	44-226	124-582

DOUBLE COLUMBIA ROUND

		50 yards	40 yards	30 yards	Totals
1879	Mrs. S. Brown	28–132	36–152	46–264	110–548
1880	Mrs. T. Davis	30–112	37–203	47–283	114–598
1881	No contest				
1882	No contest				
1883	Mrs. M. C. Howell	46–272	48–316	48–352	142–940
1884	No contest				
1885	Mrs. M. C. Howell	46–232	48–276	48–334	142–842
1886	Mrs. M. C. Howell	47–283	48–284	48–326	143–893
1887	Mrs. A. M. Phillips	46–286	48–318	48–376	142–980
1888	Mrs. A. M. Phillips	45–255	48–300	48–346	141–901
1889	Mrs. A. M. Phillips	47–267	48–320	48–358	143–945
1890	Mrs. M. C. Howell	48–292	48–320	48–354	144–966
1891	Mrs. M. C. Howell	42–224	47–259	48–330	137–813
1892	Mrs. M. C. Howell	44–206	48–282	48–330	140–818
1893	Mrs. M. C. Howell	45–233	48–302	48–344	141–879
1894	Mrs. A. Kern	39–169	38–312	47–291	124–666
1895	Mrs. M. C. Howell	45–281	48–332	48–356	141–969
1896	Mrs. M. C. Howell	48–290	48–316	48–384	144–990
1897	Mrs. J. S. Barker	42–190	45–237	48–320	135–747
1898	Mrs. M. C. Howell	45–247	45–305	48–362	140–914
1899	Mrs. M. C. Howell	45–251	48–292	48–342	141–885
1900	Mrs. M. C. Howell	47–265	47–303	48–340	142–908
1901	Mrs. C. S. Woodruff	37–177	42–198	40–252	119–627
1902	Mrs. M. C. Howell	45–215	48–282	48–352	141–849
1903	Mrs. M. C. Howell	45–233	47–303	48–276	140–862
1904	Mrs. M. C. Howell	45–245	48–274	48–348	141–867
1905	Mrs. M. C. Howell	47–253	47–305	48–352	142–910
1906	Miss E. C. Cooke	32–146	33–141	47–249	112–536
1907	Mrs. M. C. Howell	47–257	48–322	48–352	143–931
1908	Miss H. A. Case	29–127	38–182	45–237	112–546
1909	Miss H. A. Case	37–171	47–241	48–320	132–732
1910	Miss L. M. Witwer	36–168	46–268	45–297	127–733
1911	Mrs. J. H. Taylor	38–168	45–231	48–332	131–731 (a)
1912	Mrs. J. H. Taylor	39–181	45–261	47–345	131–787
1913	Mrs. L. C. Smith	29–107	40–204	47–263	116–574 (b)
1914	Mrs. B. P. Gray	47–239	48–258	48–342	143–839
1915	Miss C. M. Wesson	48–294	48–328	48–356	144–998
1916	Miss C. M. Wesson	43–191	48–302	48–354	139–847

(a) Same as Miss Witwer, married during the interim.
(b) Mrs. Smith won by points, Mrs. P. S. Fletcher making 114 hits, 586 score.

RANK OF THE WINNERS OF THE DOUBLE NATIONAL ROUND

		Times Winner	Average Winning Scores	Highest Winning Score
1.	Mrs. A. M. Phillips	3	127–675	133–713
2.	Miss C. M. Wesson	2	127–645	130–708
3.	Miss J. V. Sullivan	1	115–629	115–629
4.	Mrs. B. P. Gray	1	127–625	127–625
5.	Mrs. M. C. Howell	17	122–606	132–756
6.	Mrs. C. S. Woodruff	1	126–604	126–604
7.	Mrs. A. Kern	1	112–580	112–580
8.	Mrs. J. S. Barker	1	112–520	112–520
9.	Miss H. A. Case	2	109–487	125–577
10.	Mrs. J. H. Taylor	2	103–460	112–524
11.	Mrs. A. H. Gibbs	2	99–421	101–449
12.	Mrs. H. Hall	1	88–416	88–416
13.	Mrs. P. S. Fletcher	1	93–377	93–377
14.	Miss E. C. Cooke	1	82–302	82–302

RANK OF THE WINNERS OF THE DOUBLE COLUMBIA ROUND

		Times Winner	Average Winning Scores	Highest Winning Score
1.	Mrs. A. M. Phillips	3	142–942	142–980
2.	Miss C. M. Wesson	2	141–923	144–998
3.	Mrs. M. C. Howell	17	142–896	144–990
4.	Mrs. B. P. Gray	1	143–839	143–839
5.	Mrs. J. H. Taylor	3	130–750	131–787
6.	Mrs. J. S. Barker	1	135–747	135–747
7.	Mrs. A. Kern	1	126–666	126–666
8.	Miss H. A. Case	2	123–629	123–629
9.	Mrs. C. S. Woodruff	1	119–627	119–627
10.	Mrs. T. Davis	1	114–598	114–598
11.	Mrs. S. Brown	1	110–548	110–548

TEAM CONTEST FOR WOMEN
(4 a side)

72 arrows at 40 yards — Hits–Score

a1882	College Hills Archery Club, Cincinnati, Ohio	182– 874
1883	Highland Archers, Wyoming, Ohio	238–1076

96 arrows at 50 yards

1884	No Contest	
1885	Highland Archers, Wyoming, Ohio	291–1321
a1886	Highland Archers, Wyoming, Ohio	167– 751
1887	Robin Hood Archery Club, Dayton, Ky.	279–1229
1888	Robin Hood Archery Club, Dayton, Ky.	263–1169
1889	Robin Hood Archery Club, Dayton, Ky.	222– 876
1890	Walnut Hills Archery Club, Cincinnati, Ohio	268–1192
1891	Walnut Hills Archery Club, Cincinnati, Ohio	238–1070
1892	No Contest	
1893	Walnut Hills Archery Club, Cincinnati, Ohio. No other team present	
1894	Potomac Archers, Washington, D. C. No other team present	
1895	No Contest	
1896	Potomac Archers, Washington, D. C.	199– 833
1897	Potomac Archers, Washington, D. C.	218– 932
1898	Walnut Hills Archery Club, Cincinnati, Ohio	231–1033
1899	Walnut Hills Archery Club, Cincinnati, Ohio. No other team present	
1900	Walnut Hills Archery Club, Cincinnati, Ohio	216– 938
1901	Highland Archers, Wyoming, Ohio	196– 864
1902	No Contest	
1903	Cincinnati Archery Association	285–1307
1904	Cincinnati Archery Association	260–1144
1905	Chicago Archery Club	162– 616
1906	Boston Archers	172– 688
1907	Chicago Archery Club	225– 819
1908	Chicago Archery Club	147– 513
1909	Chicago Archery Club	277–1295
1910	Chicago Archery Club	315–1517
1911	Chicago Archery Club	201– 861
1912	Boston Archers	248–1078
1913	Newton Archers, Newton Centre, Mass.	231–1083
1914	Wayne Archers, Wayne, Pa.	295–1405
1915	No Contest	
1916	Wayne Archers, Wayne, Pa.	250–1088

(a) 3 a side.

FLIGHT SHOOT FOR WOMEN

		Yards	Inches
1882	Mrs. Frye, Williamsport, Pa.	162	
1883	No contest		
1884	No contest		
1885	No contest		
1886	Mrs. A. M. Phillips, Battle Creek, Mich.	183	
1887	Mrs. A. M. Phillips, Battle Creek, Mich.	175	24
1888	Miss E. C. Cooke, Washington, D. C.	180	
1889	Mrs. A. Kern, Dayton, Ohio	210	12
1890	Mrs. A. Kern, Dayton, Ohio	189	6
1891	Miss E. C. Cooke, Washington, D. C.	211	12
1892	Mrs. J. G. Graf, Walnut Hills, Ohio	151	
1893	Miss M. E. Strong, Cincinnati, Ohio	187	
1894	Miss E. C. Cooke, Washington, D. C.	178	6
1895	Mrs. J. S. Barker, Washington, D. C.	197	
1896	Miss E. C. Cooke, Washington, D. C.	182	
1897	Miss E. C. Cooke, Washington, D. C.	172	
1898	No contest		
1899	Mrs. A. Kern, Dayton, Ohio	211	
1900	Mrs. M. C. Howell, Norwood, Ohio	141	
1901	Miss Georgie Clark, Wyoming, Ohio	195	
1902	Miss E. C. Cooke, Washington, D. C.	190	
1903	Miss Mabel Taylor, Cincinnati, Ohio	174	
1904	Miss Mabel Taylor, Cincinnati, Ohio	219	
1905	No contest		
1906	Mrs. E. W. Frentz, Melrose, Mass.	197	
1907	Mrs. Amelia Barbe, Chicago	147	
1908	Mrs. W. G. Valentine, Chicago	139	
1909	Mrs. E. W. Frentz, Melrose, Mass.	188	
1910	Miss L. M. Witwer, Chicago	162	
1911	Miss F. M. Patrick, Oak Park, Ill.	189	
1912	Mrs. G. P. Bryant, Melrose, Mass.	229	24
1913	Mrs. G. P. Bryant, Melrose, Mass.	251	$\frac{4}{16}$
1914	Mrs. E. W. Frentz, Melrose, Mass.	220	29½
1915	No contest, on account of rain		
1916	Miss C. M. Wesson, Cotuit, Mass.	204	33

The following tables show the places where the Annual Tournaments of the National Archery Association have been held and the number of contestants in each.

		Men	Women	Total
1879	Chicago	69	20	89
1880	Buffalo, N. Y.	35	11	46
1881	Brooklyn, N. Y.	57	19	76
1882	Chicago	31	13	44
1883	Cincinnati	42	27	69
1884	Pullman, Ill.	15	1	16
1885	Eaton, Ohio	22	17	39
1886	Chautauqua, N. Y.	11	12	23
1887	Washington, D. C.	28	18	46
1888	Dayton, Ohio	35	21	56
1889	Dayton, Ohio	27	24	51
1890	Norwood, Ohio	23	15	38
1891	Natural Bridge, Va.	16	12	28
1892	Fortress Monroe, Va.	18	5	23
1893	Dayton, Ohio	24	8	32
1894	Washington, D. C.	11	7	18
1895	Dayton, Ohio	20	4	24
1896	White Sulphur Springs, Va.	6	5	11
1897	Washington, D. C	6	5	11
1898	Wyoming, Ohio	13	6	19
1899	Norwood, Ohio	10	6	16
1900	Cincinnati	13	6	19
1901	Cincinnati	14	7	21
1902	Mountain Lake Park, Md.	13	5	18
1903	Niagara Falls, N. Y.	15	6	21
1904	St. Louis	22	6	28
1905	Chicago	34	7	41
1906	Boston	14	5	19
1907	Chicago	26	10	36
1908	Chicago	25	8	33
1909	Chicago	20	16	36
1910	Chicago	23	16	39
1911	Chicago	17	15	32
1912	Boston	19	12	31
1913	Boston	25	10	35
1914	Haverford, Pa.	34	18	52
1915	Chicago	19	8	27
1916	Jersey City, N. J.	18	9	27

CHAPTER X

Report of the 38th Annual Tournament of the National Archery Association, Held at Hudson County Park, Jersey City, N. J. on August 22, 23, 24 and 25th, 1916

By James Duff

FOR the first time in a period of 30 years the above Association wandered from the beaten track, and honored the famous Scottish Archers of Jersey City with the housing of the national event. The care of the Tournament was placed in the hands of a capable Executive Committee, with James Duff as President, and Robert McNeil as Secretary, and all who participated in that year's gathering declare that there was little room for improvement. The care of the archers themselves was ideal, the weather almost perfection, and the fine grounds, granted by the Hudson County Park Commissioners, everything that the most particular archer could demand.

Naturally where a scare-heading of Infantile Paralysis, was staring one in the face it was not to be expected that any record breaking attendance was to be looked for, but despite that great drawback, over 30 shooters took part in the Tournament, and during the week produced something more than ordinary archery. The shooting was of a very high order.

On Monday evening a deputation of the Jersey Club, paid a visit to the Fairmount Hotel, and there received the visiting archers who had already arrived. On Tuesday evening the members of the National Archery Association were received by invitation at the head quarters of Clan McLeod O. S. C. of whom President Duff is the Chief; and there spent a happy evening in forgetting points of aims, targets, etc., until the clock reminded them that even the tireless archer requires a little sleep if he desires to make any show. Speeches were plentiful if short and sweet, and a social hour of song made all feel as though the visit to Jersey City was well repaid.

The annual business meeting was held at the same place as the archers had selected

Photo. by Paul Thompson

National Tournament, N. A. A., Jersey City, N. J., 1916

for headquarters, and this year it was greatly to the credit of the ladies that they turned out in goodly numbers, and took an active part in the business of the Association. Among the principal items of business brought up for discussion was the publication of a complete book on archery by the Association members, and as this work is well advanced, and will not deal in the ancient fiction of the sport but will be a book of record and information to the beginner as well as the man who knows it all, there should be quite a demand for the work.

A fitting wind up to a glorious week of pleasure was the banquet at Fairmount Hotel, J. C. on Friday evening. Something of an innovation was observed when headed by a piper, some forty fully Highland dressed Scots made their entry into the dining hall, in honor of the trust the Association had placed in their fellow members. The evening was spent in distribution of prizes, speeches short and snappy and some songs rendered by the high talented artists, the Hamilton Brothers. All was so harmonious that every one felt that it was too bad when the President called for a last standing hand clasp and a verse of Auld Lang Syne. It is hoped that the wishes of the local club will not be forgotten, when we all sing "Will Ye No Come Back Again."

The following are records of the week's work at the range and the winners.

DOUBLE YORK ROUND

	100 yards	80 yards	60 yards	Total	Golds
Dr. R. P. Elmer	49–207	39–187	23–139	111– 533	13
Wayne, Pa.	41–183	35–177	23–127	99– 487	8
	90–390	74–364	46–266	210–1020	21
James S. Jiles	32–114	28–132	20– 92	80– 338	3
Pittsburgh	32–160	36–162	24–144	92– 466	12
	64–274	64–294	44–236	172– 804	15
Homer S. Taylor	37–155	31–139	20–104	88– 398	13
Greenfield, Mass.	38–150	33–131	22– 98	93– 379	8
	75–305	64–270	42–202	181– 777	21
Dr. O. L. Hertig	30–116	32–132	23–113	84– 361	8
Pittsburgh	21–121	33–147	18– 88	72– 356	6
	51–237	65–279	41–201	157– 717	14
C. E. Dallin	30–108	28–144	20–104	78– 356	7
Arlington Heights, Mass.	26– 92	33–149	23–111	82– 352	8
	56–200	61–293	43–215	160– 708	15
G. Phillips Bryant	27– 95	30–132	18– 92	75– 319	4
Melrose, Mass.	29–105	38–188	21– 99	88– 392	7
	56–200	68–320	39–191	163– 711	11

38th Annual Tournament

	100 yards	80 yards	60 yards	Total	Golds
James Duff	19– 85	29–123	21–101	69– 309	3
Jersey City	23– 99	25–117	20–102	68– 318	4
	42–184	54–240	41–203	137– 627	7
W. P. Douthitt	22–108	15– 63	14– 72	37– 243	5
Pittsburgh	28– 86	32–104	15– 69	75– 259	1
	50–194	47–167	29–141	112– 502	6
Dr. E. I. Cole	11– 39	26–108	12– 52	49– 199	4
Ossining, N. Y.	6– 24	16– 68	14– 68	36– 160	2
	17– 63	42–176	26–120	85– 359	6
B. P. Gray	8– 20	15– 63	14– 72	37– 155	1
Newton Centre, Mass.	18– 68	15– 61	10– 54	43– 183	3
	26– 88	30–124	24–126	80– 338	4
F. T. Leport	11– 29	11– 45	14– 60	36– 134	2
Kansas City, Mo.	12– 40	19– 75	16– 58	47– 173	1
	23– 69	30–120	30–118	83– 307	3
S. G. McMeen	7– 31	11– 29	7– 23	25– 83	1
Columbus, Ohio	10– 30	10– 50	13– 55	33– 135	2
	17– 61	21– 79	20– 78	58– 218	3
Hurlbut A. Ives	6– 36	8– 26	6– 12	20– 74	0
Boston	4– 18	7– 21	10– 30	21– 69	1
	10– 54	15– 47	16– 42	41– 143	1

DOUBLE AMERICAN ROUND

	60 yards	50 yards	40 yards	Total	Golds
Dr. R. P. Elmer	27–155	29–175	30–202	86– 532	13
Wayne, Pa.	27–151	30–184	30–198	87– 533	17
	54–306	59–359	60–400	173–1065	30

	60 yards	50 yards	40 yards	Total	Golds
James S. Jiles	28–160	30–174	29–181	87– 515	13
Pittsburgh	26–150	30–178	30–200	86– 528	13
	54–310	60–352	59–381	173–1043	26
James Duff	28–134	29–183	30–200	87– 517	15
Jersey City	26–138	28–176	28–176	84– 490	16
	54–272	57–359	58–376	171–1007	31
Homer S. Taylor	22–106	27–155	30–194	79– 455	10
Greenfield, Mass.	27–135	29–171	29–163	85– 469	13
	49–241	56–326	59–357	164– 924	23
Dr. O. L. Hertig	27–139	30–144	29–171	86– 454	11
Pittsburgh	25–115	27–117	29–151	81– 383	7
	52–254	57–261	58–322	167– 837	18
G. Phillips Bryant	22– 84	27–135	29–197	78– 416	10
Melrose, Mass.	19– 87	25–123	29–189	73– 399	17
	41–171	52–258	58–386	151– 815	27
W. P. Douthitt	18– 70	28–128	27–157	73– 355	11
Pittsburgh	23–129	26–124	28–142	77– 395	5
	41–199	54–252	55–299	150– 750	16
F. T. Leport	18– 91	26–144	29–131	73– 366	7
Kansas City, Mo.	21– 86	24– 92	29–181	74– 359	9
	39–177	50–236	58–312	147– 725	16
C. E. Dallin	27–125	25–133	30–140	82– 398	6
Arlington Heights, Mass.	21– 79	23– 95	29–147	73– 321	5
	48–204	48–228	59–287	155– 719	11
John McRae	20– 76	27–133	29–143	76– 352	5
Jersey City	21– 87	26–130	28–142	75– 359	5
	41–163	53–263	57–285	151 711	10

38th Annual Tournament

	60 yards	50 yards	40 yards	Total	Golds
Dr. H. G. Goldberg	16– 56	22– 90	29–137	67– 283	3
Philadelphia	22– 84	25–115	29–167	76– 366	7
	38–140	47–205	58–304	143– 649	10
Dr. E. I. Cole	16– 56	24– 98	27–171	67– 326	11
Ossining, N. Y.	14– 76	24–100	28–130	66– 306	5
	30–132	48–198	55–301	133– 631	16
Robert W. McNeil	21– 83	26– 96	28–128	75– 307	4
Jersey City	15– 57	26– 92	28–116	69– 265	1
	36–140	52–188	56–244	144– 572	5
Hurlburt A. Ives	14– 60	21– 99	24–116	59– 275	3
Boston	15– 67	17– 71	23– 95	55– 233	3
	29–127	38–170	47–211	114– 508	6
Burton P. Gray	16– 64	17– 67	23– 95	56– 226	3
Boston	19– 91	18– 72	20– 88	57– 251	5
	35–155	35–139	43–183	113– 477	8
S. G. McMeen	3– 13	15– 75	16– 64	34– 152	3
Columbus, Ohio	9– 23	16– 69	20–122	45– 214	3
	12– 36	31–144	36–186	79– 366	6
Dr. Edward F. Corson	11– 27	16– 56	25–110	52– 193	3
Cynwyd, Pa.	10– 28	18– 75	19– 69	47– 172	1
	21– 55	34–131	44–179	99– 365	4
William McOwen	11– 51	18– 72	14– 42	43– 165	4
Jersey City	8– 18	15– 61	18– 72	41– 151	3
	19– 69	33–133	32–114	84– 316	7

Championship Scores

According to the Constitution the championship shall be determined by adding together the hits and scores of the Double American and Double York Rounds. Figuring on this basis we have the following results:

1.	Elmer	2468
2.	Jiles	2192
3.	Taylor	2046
4.	Duff	1942
5.	Hertig	1876
6.	Bryant	1840
7.	Dallin	1742
8.	Douthitt	1426
9.	Leport	1262
10.	Cole	1208
11.	Gray	1008
12.	Ives	806
13.	McMeen	721

Others shot only one Double Round.

Handicap Prizes

Handicap prizes were offered to the archers who showed the greatest improvement in the second half of each double round.

Handicap York Round, won by James S. Jiles.

Handicap American Round, won by Dr. H. G. Goldberg.

1916 JERSEY CITY, N. J.

MEN'S TEAM ROUND SCORES

96 arrows at 60 yards

Keystone Archers	1st 24	2nd 24	3rd 24	4th 24	TOTAL
Dr. Elmer	23–129	24–138	22–100	24–126	93– 493
W. D. Douthitt	21– 93	20– 92	17– 59	21– 99	79– 343
J. S. Jiles	21– 93	22– 92	21– 99	19– 91	83– 375
Dr. Hertig	20–102	23– 89	22– 92	22– 88	87– 371
	85–417	89–411	82–350	86–404	342–1582
Boston Archers					
Homer Taylor	22–114	22– 96	21–103	22–104	87– 417
Burton P. Gray	16– 60	18– 68	13– 51	15– 65	62– 244
Cyrus E. Dallin	17– 71	14– 46	13– 49	17– 73	61– 239
G. P. Bryant	21–103	23–113	22–116	22–102	88– 434
	76–348	77–323	69–319	76–244	298–1334
Jersey City Archers					
Jas. Duff	20– 92	22– 82	17– 81	21– 75	80– 330
R. W. McNeil	12– 44	15– 71	12– 50	17– 69	56– 234
John Macrae	18– 84	19– 80	17– 76	15– 59	71– 299
Dr. Cole	18– 82	19– 83	19– 85	19– 79	75– 333
	68–302	75–316	65–292	72–282	282–1196
Shooting Independently					
H. Ives, Boston	6– 30	5– 15	10– 40	11– 41	32– 126
F. Leport, Kansas City	15– 57	18– 60	17– 83	16– 62	66– 262
Wm. McOwan, Jersey City	5– 21	10– 44	8– 32	10– 36	33– 133
S. G. McMeen, Columbus	14– 58	14– 48	8– 20	10– 50	46– 176
	40–166	47–167	43–175	47–186	177– 697

FLIGHT SHOOT FOR MEN

Won by George Phillips Bryant.
Distance 289 yards, 2 feet, 4 inches.
This is only 8 inches short of the record by Maxson.

DOUBLE NATIONAL ROUND

	60 yards	50 yards	Total	Golds
Miss Cynthia M. Wesson	37–177	24–120	61–297	5
Cotuit, Mass.	43–179	20–106	63–285	5
	80–356	44–226	124–582	10
Miss Norma Pierce	35–119	23–109	58–228	4
Boston	40–172	23–121	63–293	5
	75–291	46–230	121–521	9
Mrs. John Dunlap, Jr.	24– 74	19– 63	43–137	1
Wayne, Pa.	26–114	10– 34	36–148	2
	50–188	29– 97	79–285	3
Miss F. Maude Dessau	18– 78	17– 65	35–143	2
Sound Beach, Conn.	23– 73	15– 61	38–134	0
	41–151	32–126	73–277	2
Miss Stella M. Ives	23– 93	16– 46	39–139	0
Roslindale, Mass.	18– 62	14– 68	32–130	2
	41–155	30–114	71–269	2
Dr. Cockett	18– 72	9– 25	27– 97	2
Cotuit, Mass.	29–109	17– 61	46–170	4
	47–181	26– 86	73–267	6
Mrs. Robert P. Elmer	16– 70	10– 38	26–108	0
Wayne, Pa.	14– 48	10– 40	24– 88	3
	30–118	20– 78	50–196	3
Mrs. F. L. Wesson	7– 15	10– 54	17– 69	3
Cotuit, Mass.	15– 51	11– 39	26– 90	0
	22– 66	21– 93	43–159	3
Miss Edna Wilson	10– 50	9– 25	19– 75	0
Chicago	11– 31	10– 26	21– 57	0
	21– 81	19– 51	40–132	0

38th Annual Tournament

DOUBLE COLUMBIA ROUND

	50 yards	40 yards	30 yards	Total	Golds
Miss Cynthia M. Wesson	21– 95	24–162	24–194	69–451	21
Cotuit, Mass.	22– 96	24–140	24–160	70–396	10
	43–191	48–302	48–354	139–847	31
Miss Norma Pierce	22– 84	20– 88	24–134	66–306	2
Boston	18– 70	21–103	24–108	63–281	8
	40–154	41–191	48–242	129–587	10
Miss F. M. Dessau	12– 60	22–114	22–128	56–302	4
Sound Beach, Conn.	20– 82	21– 91	21–109	62–282	4
	32–142	43–205	43–237	118–584	8
Mrs. John Dunlap, Jr.	17– 63	22–108	23–137	62–308	3
Wayne, Pa.	15– 53	21–113	22–100	58–266	4
	32–116	43–221	45–237	120–574	7
Mrs. Robert P. Elmer	16– 62	20–102	23–109	59–273	2
Wayne, Pa.	11– 45	13–159	18– 92	42–196	1
	27–107	33–161	41–201	101–469	3
Miss Stella M. Ives	15– 75	17–104	21–129	54–308	10
Roslindale, Mass.	9– 27	15– 57	19– 65	43–149	1
	24–102	33–161	40–194	97–457	11
Dr. Cockett	16– 72	11– 41	22–100	49–213	2
Cotuit, Mass.	10– 58	14– 56	23–127	47–241	4
	26–130	25– 97	45–227	96–454	6
Mrs. F. L. Wesson	7– 17	9– 31	21–115	37–163	3
Cotuit, Mass.	10– 32	10– 38	15– 43	35–113	2
	17– 49	19– 69	36–158	72–276	5
Miss Edna Wilson	1– 1	12– 56	16– 84	29–141	3
Chicago	9– 27	9– 35	19– 73	37–135	0
	10– 28	21– 91	35–157	66–276	3

CHAMPIONSHIP SCORES

1. Miss Wesson   1692
2. Miss Pierce   1358
3. Mrs. Dunlap   1058
4. Miss Dessau   1052
5. Miss Ives   894
6. Dr. Cockett   890
7. Mrs. Elmer   816
8. Mrs. Wesson   550
9. Miss Wilson   514

1916 JERSEY CITY, N. J.

WOMEN'S TEAM ROUND

96 arrows at 50 yds.

Wayne Archers	1st 24	2nd 24	3rd 24	4th 24	TOTAL
Cynthia Wesson	21–105	21–105	22–118	23–125	87– 453
Mrs. Dunlop	16– 68	11– 37	15– 59	12– 44	54– 208
Mrs. Elmer	12– 52	7– 19	10– 40	12– 48	41– 159
Dr. Cockett	14– 46	20– 72	16– 64	18– 86	68– 268
	63–271	59–233	63–281	65–303	250–1088

Boston Archers	1st 24	2nd 24	3rd 24	4th 24	TOTAL
Norma Pierce	18– 90	21– 91	19– 81	15– 63	73– 325
F. M. Dessau	17– 91	15– 69	12– 56	14– 70	58– 286
Mrs. Wesson	7– 25	11– 47	9– 25	16– 74	43– 171
Stella M. Ives	14– 62	22– 88	16– 64	19– 73	71– 287
	54–268	69–295	56–226	64–280	245–1069

WOMEN'S FLIGHT SHOOT

	yards	feet	inches
Won by Miss Cynthia Wesson			
Distance	204	2	9

Wand Shoot at 40 yards
Won by Miss Wesson   2 hits
Dr. Cockett   1 hit

38th Annual Tournament

The Women's Handicap Contests were shot out in full, as separate events.

Winner of Handicap National, Miss Dessau. Made 188, given 152, total 340.

Winner of Handicap Columbia, Mrs. Wesson. Made 197, given 286, total 483.

1916 JERSEY CITY, N. J.

CLAN MCLEOD NO. 70 O.S.C. NOVELTY COMPETITION CUP

The competition for this trophy—presented by the Jersey City Branch of the Order of Scottish Clans—took place on Friday afternoon. The Novelty Competition took the form of a duck shoot. The figure of a duck painted black, with eye and breast painted white, was placed on the target in such manner as to cover the gold. Forty-eight arrows were shot at forty yards and an eye counted 3, a breast 2 and any other part of the body 1. Hits were added to score in final computation. The contest resulted in a tie of 28 each between Mr. Leport and Mr. Duff. Six additional rounds of 6 arrows each were shot without a decision. In the seventh round, the hits nearest to the duck were counted and Mr. Duff was declared victor by one hit.

1916 JERSEY CITY, N. J.
JILES CUP
IMPROVED TOURNAMENT SCORE

J. S. Jiles	1915	1241	
	1916	1847	606
J. Duff	1915	1309	
	1916	1770	461
Dr. Elmer	1915	1682	
	1916	2085	403
H. S. Taylor	1914	1406	
	1916	1701	295
W. D. Douthitt	1915	1047	
	1916	1277	230
C. E. Dallin	1914	1247	
	1916	1419	172
Dr. Hertig	1915	1389	
	1916	1553	164
Miss Norma Pierce	1914	981	
	1916	1108	127
G. P. Bryant	1914	1445	
	1916	1526	81
E. I. Cole	1914	1100	
	1916	990	
Mrs. R. P. Elmer	1914	769	
	1916	665	
Mrs. Wesson	1915	683	
	1916	435	
Miss Wesson	1915	1706	
	1916	1429	
B. P. Gray	1914	1257	
	1916	815	

Combined scores in Double American and Double York Rounds, for men, and Double Columbia and Double National for women. Archer showing greatest improvement over his or her last tournament score wins. No score more than ten years old to be considered.

Jiles cup, won by J. S. Jiles.

1916 JERSEY CITY, N. J.

WOMEN

Christian Science Monitor Shield for the most hits in the Double National and Double Columbia Rounds. At the end of five years, from 1912, to become the property of the highest of five winners.

1912	Boston, won by Mrs. Witwer Taylor, Chicago	243 hits
1913	Boston, won by Mrs. P. S. Fletcher, Chicago	207 "
1914	Haverford, won by Mrs. B. P. Gray, Boston	270 "
1915	Chicago, won by Miss C. M. Wesson, Bryn Mawr	274 "
1916	Jersey City, won by Miss C. M. Wesson, Bryn Mawr	262 "

Awarded to Miss Wesson on score made at Chicago in 1915.

Dr. Robert P. Elmer.
    Champion Archer of the United States.
    Awarded Dallin Medal in gold.
          "   York Round Medal.
          "   American Round Medal.
          "   Maurice Thompson Medal.
          "   Potomac Medal.
          "   Chicago Cup.

Having won the Chicago Cup for the third time it became the permanent property of Dr. Elmer.

James S. Jiles.
    Second in Championship Contest.
    Awarded Dallin Medal in silver.
          "   80 yards range medal.
          "   Jiles Cup.

As Captain of the Keystone Archers, Mr. Jiles was made custodian of the Pearsall Bugle.

Homer S. Taylor.
    Third in Championship Contest.
    Awarded Dallin medal in bronze.
          "   100 yards range medal.
          "   Spalding medal.

James Duff.
> Awarded 50 yards range medal. Medal missing since 1914 and not presented.
> Awarded Clan McLeod Cup, for the Duck Shoot.

Dr. Hertig.
> Awarded 60 yards range medal.

G. P. Bryant.
> Awarded 40 yards range medal.
> " Ovington Beaker.

F. E. Leport.
> Awarded Duff Gold Medal for highest score in the Team Shoot made by an archer who was not a member of a team.

John MacRae.
> Awarded the Duff Arrow.

S. G. McMeen.
> Awarded the Elmer Wooden Spoon.

Miss Cynthia M. Wesson.
> Champion Woman Archer of the United States.
> Awarded Dallin Medal in gold.
> " National Round Medal.
> " Columbia Round Medal.
> " Weston Trophy.

Made custodian of the Peacock Cup which was won by the Wayne Archers.

Awarded the Christian Science Monitor Shield to keep.

Miss Norma Pierce.

Second in Women's Championship Contest.
Awarded Dallin Medal in silver.
" 60 yards range medal.

Mrs. John Dunlap, Jr.

Third in Women's Championship Contest.
Awarded Dallin Medal in bronze.
" 40 yards range medal.

Miss F. M. Dessau.

Awarded 50 yards range medal.
" Maid Marian Arrow.
" Beach Brooch, by virtue of being the youngest woman present.

Dr. Marguerite Cocket.

Awarded the 30 yard range medal.

CHAPTER XI

THE EASTERN ARCHERY ASSOCIATION

By Dr. Robert P. Elmer

THE Eastern Archery Association was formed in 1879, the same year as the National Archery Association, for the purpose, stated in its constitution, of associating under one general management and head, the various archery societies of the Eastern United States. Membership was not held by individuals, but by clubs, the following being the founders of the association:

The Pequosette Archers	Watertown, Mass.
The Waltham Archers	Waltham, Mass.
The Orchard Archers	Fitchburg, Mass.
The Oritani Archers	Hackensack, N. J.
The West Newton Archery Club	West Newton, Mass.
The Toxarchs	Newton, Mass.
The Greenfield Archers	Greenfield, Mass.
The Maple Grove Archers	Springfield, Mass.
The Massasoit Bowmen	Springfield, Mass.

The constitution adopted was identical with that of the National Archery Association, except for the proper names.

Inasmuch as all but one of the charter societies was from Masschusetts, the first tournament was held at Beacon Park, Boston, on the 25th and 26th of September, 1879, a few weeks after the first National Tournament had been held at Chicago.

The following clubs were represented:

	Men	Women	
The Pequosette Archers	6	4	Watertown, Mass.
The Waltham Archers	1	1	Waltham, Mass.
The Oritani Archers	5	0	Hackensack, N. J.
The West Newton A. C.	5	4	West Newton, Mass.
The Brooklyn A. C.	5	0	Brooklyn, N. Y.
The Toxophilites	6	0	Lewiston, Maine
The Cedarwoods	4	0	Poughkeepsie, N. Y.
Robin Hood Archers	1	0	Nyack, N. Y.
Ellenville A. C.	Not known		Ellenville, N. Y.

The best scores were:

Double American Round (Championship)
1. E. R. Dwight, Watertown   122–556
2. H. Ennis, Poughkeepsie   113–535
3. J. O. Blake, Chicago (with Brooklyn)   120–522

Men's Team, Single American Round
  Brooklyn A. C.
    J. G. Johnston   58–246
    J. O. Blake   46–246
    Major A. G. Constable   38–166
    Dr. D. F. Wemple   33–129

Double Columbia Round (Championship)
1. Miss Silsbee, Watertown   86–406
2. Miss Allen, West Newton   94–366
3. Miss Walker, Watertown   63–313

Women's Team, Single Columbia Round
  Pequosette Archers
    Miss Silsbee   34–156
    Miss Walker   25–125
    Mrs. Shackford   25–143
                                                  ——————
                                                  84–424

The second tournament was held at Ridge Hill Farms, Wellesley, Mass., on September 1st and 2nd, 1880. Ten archery clubs were represented by 31 men and 9 women.

Best scores:

Double York Round (Championship)
  1. L. L. Peddinghaus, Marietta, Ohio   127–519
  2. F. H. Brackett, Roxbury, Mass.   128–474
  3. W. G. Morse, Poughkeepsie   105–395

Men's Team Round (72 arrows at 60 yards)
  Hawthorne Archers, Roxbury
    F. H. Brackett   61–221
    Howard Brackett   47–207
    James Dwight   48–192
    F. D. Ritzer   42–126
                                                 ——————
                                                 198–746

Double Columbia Round (Championship)
  1. Miss Abba Agar, Jamaica Plain, Mass.   108–526
  2. Miss E. L. Magee, Watertown, Mass.   63–245
  3. Miss Allen, West Newton, Mass.   58–242

Women's Team Round (72 arrows at 50 yards)
  Jamaica Plain Archers
    Miss A. Agar   46–178
    Miss J. Agar   43–171
    Miss J. Sprague   40–156
                                                 ——————
                                                 129–505

The records of the association from this time until 1911 are lost. It is known that tournaments were held, but various inquiries have failed, as yet, to elicit any satisfactory information concerning them.

In a letter to Dr. Weston, in 1914, Mr. Will H. Thompson wrote, "We came near wrecking archery at one time over the attempt to change the value of the colors on the target to 1, 2, 3, 4 and 5. The Eastern Archery Association adopted the silly change for no technical reason whatever."

In the Spalding Official Archery Guide, written by Dr. Weston in 1909, he states, "In recent years the members of the Eastern Archery Association have shot on their local ranges, and reported the scores to the Secretary. This has constituted the annual meeting."

Let us hope that these records may yet be found.

In the fall of 1911, H. B. Richardson, President of the National Archery Association, issued a call to all archers in the Eastern United States to hold a tournament on November 11th, to compete for the championship medals of the Eastern Archery Association, which were then in the possession of Wallace Bryant. Those archers who could do so were expected to shoot on the Playgrounds at Newton Centre, Mass., but those who could not be there were allowed to shoot on any range and send their scores in to Mr. Richardson to be recorded.

Eight men and seven women competed at Newton Centre and seven men at Wayne, Pa. No other localities were represented.

Inasmuch as the original constitution of the Eastern Archery Association was temporarily lost, the rules of this and the succeeding tournaments were modelled as closely as possible on those of the National Archery Association.

Best scores:

Single York Round
1. Wallace Bryant, Boston   97-443
2. G. P. Bryant, Melrose   87-421
3. H. B. Richardson, Boston   78-310

Single American Round
1. G. P. Bryant   88-464
2. Wallace Bryant   86-464
3. H. B. Richardson   84-426

Single National Round
1. Miss Helen Hutchinson   65-323
2. Miss F. Bogert   45-191
3. Miss H. Davis   45-187

The tournament for 1912 was also held as a mail-match, the date being set for October 12th, thereby setting the precedent of having the tournament either on Columbus Day or as near it as possible. The list of entries was much longer than in the previous year, there being 24 men and 18 women. Among the former were six Scottish-American Archers from Jersey City and several individuals from widely scattered points. Six men and seven women were from western cities and so were not considered eligible for the prizes although their scores added interest to the competition.

Best scores:

Single York Round
1. G. P. Bryant — 101–467
2. W. H. Wills, New York City — 89–347
3. H. B. Richardson — 75–327

Single American Round
1. G. P. Bryant — 88–550
2. G. L. Nichols, Chicago — 89–549
3. Dr. Hertig, Pittsburgh — 86–476

Single National Round
1. Miss Helen Hutchinson, Boston — 48–210
2. Miss F. M. Patrick, Brooklyn — 46–192
3. Miss C. Wesson, Cotuit, Mass. — 39–165

Single Columbia Round
1. Mrs. Witwer-Taylor, Chicago — 71–449
2. Miss H. Hutchinson (Winner) — 68–378
3. Mrs. G. Wallace, Des Moines — 64–318

The success attending these mail-matches made it seem advisable to adopt normal tournament conditions for the contest in 1913, so an invitation was given by the Wayne Archers for a meeting in that place on the 4th of July.

The tournament was held in connection with other field sports and was witnessed by fully two thousand people. Different ranges were used in the morning and afternoon but on neither of them was there space enough to shoot the York Round. Only the Double American Round was shot, there being no women contestants. Eighteen men, coming from seven different places, were present.

Best scores:

Double American Round

1. Dr. Elmer, Wayne	88–	528
	86–	504
	174–	1032
2. A. C. Hale, Wayne	82–	404
	84–	492
	166–	896
3. Dr. Hertig, Pittsburgh	82–	398
	83–	439
	165–	837

In 1914 the tournament was held in Jersey City, on the invitation of the Scottish-American Archers. The shooting filled three days, October 8th, 9th and 10th, giving ample time for the full Double York and Double American Rounds.

Best scores:

Double York Round
1. James S. Jiles, Pittsburgh   154–722
2. Dr. Hertig   165–653
3. H. S. Taylor, Buffalo   153–695

Although the best score was made by Jiles, the Championship was awarded to Hertig on points, viz:

Hertig		Jiles		Taylor
Total hits	2	Total score	2	
Hits at 100	1	Score at 80	1	Half hits at 60 ½
Score at 100	1	Score at 60	1	
Hits at 80	1	Half hits at 60	½	
	5		4½	

Double American Round
1. James Duff, Jersey City   165–963
2. James Jiles   162–962
3. Dr. Hertig   158–898

Handicap medals for both events were won by McRae, of Jersey City.

In 1915 a two day tournament, on October 8th and 9th, was to be held at Newton Centre,

Mass., but the weather conditions were so bad that the competition had to be confined to the second day. A few archers shot for practice in the afternoon of the first day and Mrs. Gray made an American round score of 84-474, which was higher than the score that won.

Twenty men and seven women took part.

Best scores:

Single York Round
1. C. E. Dallin, Arlington Heights, Mass.   91-417
2. H. S. Taylor, Buffalo   72-360
3. G. P. Bryant   74-320

Single American Round
1. C. E. Dallin   87-471
2. Dr. H. B. Richardson   82-424
3. James Duff   78-402

Double National Round
1. Mrs. B. P. Gray, Newton Centre   116-558
2. Mrs. G. P. Bryant, Melrose   87-377
3. Miss Ives, Roslindale, Mass.   80-340

Double Columbia Round
1. Mrs. B. P. Gray   139-797
2. Miss Norma Pierce, Boston   122-624
3. Mrs. G. P. Bryant   123-581

Since the revival of the tournaments of the Eastern Archery Association, each had been a more successful occasion than the one of the previous year. That of 1916 was held at Newton Centre on October 12th and

13th and was considered, by archers of experience, to have been the best of all. The full scores follow:

Double York Round

1.	James Duff	90-394	81-365	171-759
2.	F. I. Peckham	81-360	59-267	140-627
3.	G. P. Bryant	62-248	74-288	136-536
4.	C. T. Switzler	63-255	64-270	127-525
5.	A. Shepherdson	63-269	59-233	122-502
6.	L. C. Smith	52-200	46-250	98-450
7.	E. J. Cole	42-176	54-218	96-394
8.	H. A. Ives	42-142	50-171	92-313
9.	S. W. Wilder	44-174	29-113a	73-287
10.	T. H. Uzzell	35-115	52-162	77-277
11.	J. C. Bushong	32-114	40-132	72-246
12.	J. P. True	24- 92	28-114	52-206
13.	J. McOwen	25- 94	32- 98	56-192
14.	Ellis Spear	27-115		27-115
15.	S. E. Hall	28- 90		28- 90

Double American Round

1.	A. Shepherdson	83-483	80-446	163-929
2.	James Duff	85-517	77-391	162-908
3.	E. W. Frentz	82-432	79-403	161-835
4.	G. P. Bryant	79-389	75-405	154-794
5.	F. I. Peckham	79-415	78-378	157-793
6.	C. T. Switzler	79-389	80-402	159-791
7.	L. C. Smith	79-381	76-396	155-777
8.	E. J. Cole	78-352	76-392	154-744
9.	H. A. Ives	76-356	77-359	153-715
10.	C. W. Dallin	79-335	74-368	153-703
11.	Elles Spear	63-237	68-366	131-603
12.	F. J. Lightbody	70-282	66-310	136-592
13.	J. C. Bushong	54-226	67-313	121-539
14.	T. H. Uzzell	58-244	63-277	121-521
15.	J. McOwen	58-270	58-228	116-498
16.	S. W. Wilder	79-409		79-409
17.	J. P. True	44-192	54-206	98-308
18.	S. E. Hall	56-260		56-260
19.	H. S. Bouker	41-161		41-161

a Second round was not finished.

In the manner prescribed by the new constitution of the National Archery Association the Champion was found by adding together the total hits and scores in both double rounds. By this method the first three men were:

    1. James Duff   2000
    2. F. I. Peckham   1717
    3. A. Shepherdson   1716

Double National Round

1.	Mrs. B. P. Gray	53-247	58-310	111-557
2.	Miss C. M. Wesson	49-209	58-266	107-475
3.	Miss S. Ives	34-138	38-148	72-286
4.	Miss N. True	34-130	31-111	65-241
5.	Miss N. Pierce	48-186		48-186
6.	Mrs. F. Wesson	25- 79	20- 84	45-163
7.	Mrs. T. H. Uzzell	19- 45	13- 73	32-122
8.	Mrs. A. Shepherdson	11- 45	11- 33	22- 78
9.	Miss Ruth Brewer	19- 69		19- 69
10.	Mrs. J. P. True	1- 5	2- 6	3- 11

Double Columbia Round

1.	Miss C. M. Wesson	67-347	70-398	137-745
2.	Mrs. B. P. Gray	70-326	68-400	138-726
3.	Miss N. True	55-283	51-223	106-506
4.	Miss S. Ives	38-198	33-143	71-341
5.	Mrs. E. W. Frentz		58-296	58-296
6.	Miss Norma Pierce			61-291
7.	Mrs. J. P. True	13- 49	32-118	45-267
8.	Mrs. T. H. Uzzell	29-115	38-138	67-253
9.	Miss Dorothy Smith	57-247		57-247
10.	Mrs. F. Wesson	24- 85	30-110	54-194
11.	Miss Ruth Brewer	20- 70	24- 98	44-168
12.	Mrs. A. Shepherdson	32-130		32-130

By totals Mrs. Gray was first with 1532. Miss Wesson got 1464.

CHAPTER XII

Best Scores of All Kinds and Feats of Skill

By Dr. Robert P. Elmer

IT HAS been the good fortune of very few archers to make their best scores at the large tournaments, so that the records of these events do not give a fair idea of what many of the contestants are capable of doing when every circumstance is favorable. Furthermore, some of the most skillful archers in the country have been so situated that they have never been able to do more than shoot by themselves or in the company of a few friends.

This article is written for the purpose of rescuing from oblivion the best scores that have been made under any conditions. Some of them can be vouched for by no one but the archer himself, but many were made in club contests or before witnesses in other ways. Wherever it is known to the editor that other people saw a score made he has mentioned the fact.

Of necessity these lists are incomplete. Without doubt there are many fine scores that the editor does not know anything about, but he has made a careful search of all the data at his disposal and he feels safe in asserting that the tabulated results form a pretty good index of the best that is in American archery.

SINGLE AMERICAN ROUND

1. E. J. Rendtorff
   Lake Forest, Ill.
   30–224
   30–228
   30–230
   ―――
   90–682
   Shot at Lake Forest, Ill., 3 P. M., Monday, 2 June, 1913, in private match with Prof. Bross Thomas. Reported *Forest & Stream*, 28 June, 1913.

2. I. W. Maxson
   Washington, D. C.
   (Died 2 July, 1916)
   30–204
   30–226
   30–240
   ―――
   90–670
   Reported by Dr. Weston. Particulars unknown.

3. Dr. R. P. Elmer
   Wayne, Pa.
   29–191
   30–222
   30–242
   ―――
   89–655
   Private practice, 17 September, 1917.

4. W. A. Clark
   Cincinnati, Ohio
   (Died 20 Oct., 1913)
   90–646
   Made in club contest of Highland Archers of Wyoming, Ohio. Score shown Dr. Elmer by Mr. Clark.

5. J. B. Siders
   Los Angeles, Cal.
   30–182
   30–220
   30–234
   ―――
   90–636
   Reported by Dr. Weston in *Christian Science Monitor*, 14 January, 1914.

6. M. Sorber   90-630   Club contest. Scored and re-
   Pittsburgh, Pa.   ported by Dr. Hertig.

7. Arthur Young   30-190   Witnessed and scored by Dr.
   San Francisco, Cal. 30-198   Pope. 25 March, 1917.
                       30-238
                       ──────
                       90-626

8. F. C. Havens   28-184   Reported by Dr. Weston, P.
   Oakland, Cal.   30-212   112 *Spalding's Guide*, 2nd Edi-
                       30-230   tion. Shot in a match.
                       ──────
                       88-626

9. W. J. Holmes   30-180   Club contest, 22 Nov., 1913.
   Pittsburgh   30-210   Scored by Dr. Hertig.
                       29-233
                       ──────
                       89-623

10. C. C. Beach   30-198   Private practice in the autumn
    Battle Creek   30-208   of 1908. Reported by Mr.
    Mich.   30-216   Beach to Dr. Weston for
    (Deceased)   ──────   publication in *Spalding's Arch-
                       90-622   ery Guide*.

11. G. P. Bryant   30-186   American Record. National
    Boston   30-200   Tournament at Boston, 1912.
                       30-232
                       ──────
                       90-618

12. H. W. Bishop   30-176   Private practice, Dec., 1912.
    Chicago   30-206   Reported in *Forest & Stream*,
                       30-236   28 Dec., 1912.
                       ──────
                       90-618

13. H. S. Taylor   90-612   Club contest, Chicago Archery
    Greenfield, Mass.   Association, 30 August, 1913.
                                Scored by Mr. Pendry.

Best Scores of All Kinds 117

14.	Dr. O. L. Hertig Pittsburgh	30–172 30–214 30–220 ――― 90–606	Club contest for the 3rd N. A. A. Mail Match, October, 1913.
15.	Miss C. M. Wesson Cotuit, Mass.	30–186 30–186 30–222 ――― 90–594	Private practice, 21 July, 1915. Reported by letter for this book.
16.	W. D. Douthitt Pittsburgh	89–579	Club contest. Scored by Dr. Hertig.
17.	G. L. Nichols Chicago	88–578	Reported by Dr. Weston.
18.	A. R. Clark Berea, Ohio	29–157 30–206 30–204 ――― 89–577	Reported by Dr. Weston.
19.	Mrs. M. C. Howell Cincinnati	28–174 30–190 30–210 ――― 88–574	Private practice, 25 July, 1883. Letter of 28 May, 1917, from Mrs. Howell.
20.	C. E. Dallin Arlington Heights, Mass.	88–574	Club contest of the Newton Archers, 10 October, 1914. Scored by L. C. Smith.
21.	J. S. Jiles Pittsburgh	90–566	Club contest Pittsburgh Archers, 9 July, 1916.
22.	Dr. C. S. Case Chicago	27–175 30–192 29–199 ――― 86–566	Reported by Dr. Weston.

23.	B. P. Gray Boston	29-155 30-198 30-212 ——— 89-565	Reported by Dr. Weston.
24.	J. Duff Jersey City	90-562	Private practice, 21 August, 1916, at Jersey City. Scored by F. .T. Leport of Kansas City, Mo.
25.	F. I. Peckham Boston	29-165 29-179 30-218 ——— 88-562	Club contest, Newton Archers, 9 July, 1914. Scored by L. C. Smith.
26.	F. E. Canfield	87-555	Reported by Dr. Weston.
27.	Mrs. B. P. Gray Newton Centre	29-147 30-196 30-210 ——— 89-553	Private practice. Scored by B. P. Gray. 26 golds.
28.	Dr. J. W. Doughty Fort Steilacoom, Wash.	89-553	Private practice.
29.	S. W. Wilder Boston	88-552	Club contest, Newton Archers.
30.	J. A. Rose Crawfordsville, Ind.	86-550	Reported by Dr. Weston
31.	Dr. H. G. Goldberg Bala, Pa.	29-159 30-184 30-206 ——— 89-549	Cynwyd Club contest, 27 July, 1915. Scored by Dr. Corson.
32.	Dr. S. T. Pope San Francisco	29-157 29-185 30-196 ——— 88-538	Private practice with Arthur Young, 24 May, 1917.

33.	F. N. Clay Newark, N. J.	30–148 28–184 30–200 ——— 86–538	Private practice.
34.	T. T. Hare Radnor, Pa.	29–153 30–172 30–206 ——— 89–531	Private practice at Radnor, Pa. Fall of 1914.
35.	Mrs. E. E. Trout Wayne, Pa.	26–150 30–186 30–192 ——— 86–528	Private practice. Scored by E. E. Trout.
36.	J. H. Pendry Chicago	84–520	Club contest, Chicago Archery Association, 1913.
37.	S. G. McMeen Columbus, Ohio	28–138 29–169 30–212 ——— 87–519	Private practice, 23 March, 1917, on the Polo Field at Honolulu. Score witnessed and checked by Mrs. McMeen.
38.	L. C. Smith Newton Centre	89–515	Reported by Dr. Weston.
39.	W. B. Worstall Zanesville, Ohio	88–514	Reported by Dr. Weston Private practice.
40.	Tacitus Hussey Des Moines, Iowa	29–147 30–164 30–196 ——— 89–507	Private practice, 3 May, 1913, Des Moines. Scored by Mrs. H. W. Turner. Mr. Hussey was 82 years old.
41.	H. L. Walker Chicago	26–146 29–173 30–188 ——— 85–507	Club contest, Chicago Archery Association, 1913.

DOUBLE AMERICAN ROUND

Rendtorff

30–200	30–246	30–234	90– 680	Private practice.
30–208	30–226	30–234	90– 668	
			180–1348	

Maxson

30–204	30–210	30–234	90– 648	Public exhibition at Washington Grove, Md., 11 July, 1890.
30–210	30–216	30–240	90– 666	
			180–1314	

Elmer

30–200	30–218	30–218	90– 636	
29–191	30–222	30–242	89– 655	
			179–1291	

W. Clark

180–1248	Club contest of Highland Archers of Wyoming, Ohio

Taylor

90– 612
90– 608
180–1220

Bryant

90– 610
87– 601
177–1211

Holmes

30–180	30–210	29–233	89– 623	Club contest, 22 Nov., 1913.
29–169	30–204	30–214	·89– 587	
			178–1210	

Bishop

29–177	30–192	30–224	89– 593	Private practice, 11 Jan., 1914. Temperature 30.
30–178	30–200	30–230	90– 608	
			179–1201	

Beach

30–172	29–191	30–222	89– 585
28–160	30–188	30–242	88– 590
			177–1175

Best Scores of All Kinds

Hertig				
30–172	30–214	30–220	90– 540	
			90– 606	
			180–1146	
Jiles			90– 566	Club contest, 9 July, 1916.
			90– 564	
			180–1130	
R. Williams			177–1129	Ohio State Championship, 1883.
Duff			90– 556	Private practice, 21 Aug. 1916. Scored by Leport and Jiles.
			90– 562	
			180–1118	
Case				
27–175	30–192	29–199	86– 566	
29–169	29–181	30–192	88– 542	
			174–1108	
Miss Wesson			554	Club contest, Scottish-American Archers, July, 1915.
			546	
			1100	
Mrs. Gray				
28–162	30–164	30–170	88– 496	Private practice. Scored by Mr. Gray.
29–147	30–196	30–210	89– 553	
			177–1049	
Mrs. Trout				
26–150	30–186	30–192	86– 528	15 and 17 Sept., 1914. Scored by Mr. Trout.
29–155	30–158	30–206	89– 519	
			175–1047	
Clay				
28–154	28–184	30–200	86– 538	
28–128	30–170	30–184	88– 482	
			174–1030	
A. Clark			177–1025	National Tournament, 1900.

DOUBLE YORK ROUND

Rendtorff
68–308	47–237	24–156	141– 799	Private practice, 1913.
68–336	48–234	24–154	140– 722	
			279–1423	

R. Williams
59–293	45–239	24–176	128– 708	August 9 and 10, 1885.
62–274	45–229	24–152	131– 655	
			259–1363	

G. P. Bryant
57–269	47–235	24–142	128– 646	Shot in club contests of
61–293	45–251	24–158	130– 702	the Newton Archers, July,
			258–1348	1912.

H. S. Taylor
56–260	44–204	23–147	123– 611	
			117– 591	
			240–1202	

W. A. Clark
			250–1192	Club contest, Highland Archers, Wyoming, Ohio.

Hertig
55–243	44–204	23–149	122– 596	Both rounds shot the same
57–245	43–199	24–134	124– 578	afternoon, Oct. 4, 1913, in competition with Mr.
			246–1174	Holmes.

Holmes
53–253	42–196	24–144	119– 593	Shot Oct. 4th and Sept.
45–183	42–204	24–144	111– 531	27th in club contests.
			230–1124	

Richardson
50–210	43–217	22–117	115– 545	American Record. National Tournament, 1910.
46–190	46–238	24–138	116– 566	
			231–1111	

Best Scores of All Kinds

Doughty
51-237	41-191	21-111	113- 539	July 26 and 27, 1913, in competition with Will Thompson.
49-203	42-212	22-120	113- 535	
			226-1074	

W. H. Thompson
41-173	44-226	23-121	108- 520	October, 1882.
50-194	43-217	24-132	117- 543	
			225-1063	

SINGLE YORK RECORD

Rendtorff
68-336 48-234 24-154 140- 722   Private practice, 1913.

R. Williams
59-293 45-239 24-176 128- 708   August 9, 1885.

G. P. Bryant
61-293 45-251 24-158 130- 702   Club contest, July, 1912.

H. S. Taylor
57-257 44-252 24-156 125- 665   Club contest, Chicago A. A., July, 1911.

Doughty
123- 635   Private practice, July, 1913.

W. A. Clark
63-247 48-204 24-136 135- 587   October 31, 1883.

Hertig
55-243 44-204 23-149 122- 596   Oct. 4, 1913, with Mr. Holmes.

Holmes
53-253 42-196 24-144 119- 593   Oct. 4, 1913, in competition with Dr. Hertig.

Elmer
49-201 42-226 24-152 115- 579   Private practice, Aug., 1911.

W. H. Wills
41-217 42-208 24-146 117- 571

Richardson					
46-190	46-238	24-138	116-566		National Tournament, 1910.
W. H. Thompson					
50-194	43-217	24-132	117-543		

Bishop	23-131	Reported by Dr. Weston.
	24-140	
	24-142	
	23-139	
	94-552	
Jiles	93-551	Club contest, Pittsburgh Archers.
Nichols	94-544	Reported by Dr. Weston.
Canfield	24-136	Reported by Dr. Weston.
	24-142	
	22-134	
	24-130	
	94-542	
Adam Gray Cincinnati	95-531	Reported by Dr. Weston.
Dr. W. C. Williams	22-122	Reported by Dr. Weston.
	23-141	
	23-135	
	21-119	
	89-517	
B. P. Gray	94-504	Club contest. Newton Archers.

MEN'S TEAM ROUND (60 yards)

Rendtorff	96-664	Private practice.
H. S. Taylor	96-638	About 1883. Mail match with F. H. Walworth, of New York. Witnessed by H. C. Carver and Dr. Weston.

Maxson	24-170 24-156 24-162 24-142 ——— 96-630	Reported by Dr. Weston.
W. A. Clark	24-176 24-148 24-146 24-148 ——— 96-618	November 25, 1897. In *Spalding's Guide*.
Elmer	24-154 21-133 24-160 24-168 ——— 93-615	Private match with A. C. Hale, Aug. 9, 1912.
A. W. Houston Evanston, Ohio	94-604	Aug., 1883. Member of team of the Highland Archers, of Wyoming, Ohio, at Ohio State Meeting.
Holmes	95-593	Club contest, Pittsburgh Archers, 1913.
Hertig	95-581	Club contest, Pittsburgh Archers, 1913.
Sorber	94-578	Club contest, Pittsburgh Archers, 1913.
Douthitt	94-574	Club contest, Pittsburgh Archers, 1913.
A. E. Spink Chicago	24-156 24-154 24-148 24-122 ——— 96-560	Reported by Dr. Weston.

C. S. Upson	24–156	Reported by Dr. Weston.
Cincinnati, Ohio	24–134	
	24–134	
	23–133	
	95–557	
Dr. H. E. Jones	24–130	Before 1914. Dr. Jones was very
Portland, Oregon	24–144	deaf and usually shot alone. Some-
	24–134	times he shot with F. S. Barnes, the
	24–148	bowyer.
	96–556	

Women's Scores

Mrs. B. P. Gray, *Newton Centre, Mass.*

In a letter from her husband, dated July 12th, 1916, Mrs. Gray's best scores were given as follows:

Single Columbia Round   21–123   Columbia Handicap. National[1]
                                    22–144   Tournament, 1914.
                                    24–174
                                    67–441

Double Columbia Round
  23–121 24–138 24–180 71–439 National Tournament, 1914
  24–118 24–120 24–162 72–400
                            143–839

This event was so closely contested that the relative position of the first three ladies, Mrs. Gray, Mrs. Trout and Miss Wesson, was decided by the last arrow.

Single National Round	70–398	Columbus Day Tournament of the Newton Archers, Newton Centre Playground, October 12, 1914.
Single American Round	29–147 30–196 30–210	Practice at Newton Centre Playground, June 22nd, 1915. Scored by Mr. Gray.
	89–553	

A Womans' Team Round mentioned in a letter of August 5th, 1914, is presumably her best. Score:

    24–138
    22–108
    22–140
    23–133
    91–519

At the Columbus Day Tournament at Newton Centre, August 12th, 1914, she won the Women's Team Round with 94–516.

MRS. M. C. HOWELL, *Norwood, Ohio.*

Mrs. Howell won the Womans' Championship 17 times, a record which probably will never be beaten.

In response to a request, Mrs. Howell kindly sent her best scores for publication in this book, writing May 28th, 1917. They follow in full:

Double National Round

    85–477   Practice. June 26th, 1883.
    46–258
    ―――――
    131–735

    88–436   Ohio State Meet. Pleasant Ridge. Charles
    47–283   Strong's grounds. August, 1904.
    ―――――
    135–719

    85–413   National Tournament. Ludlow Grove, Cincinnati.
    47–277   July 10th, 1883.
    ―――――
    132–690

    82–402   Practice.
    44–278
    ―――――
    126–680

Single National Round

    47–291   Practice. June 14th, 1884.
    24–148
    ―――――
    71–439

    47–261   Practice. June 12th, 1884.
    24–144
    ―――――
    71–405

    45–249   Practice. June 3rd, 1884.
    24–146
    ―――――
    69–395

Double Columbia Round

    46–312   "My best practice score." June 30th, 1884.
    48–358   Shot in one afternoon.
    48–378
    ―――――
    142–1048

Best Scores of All Kinds

24-150	24-150	24-192	72-492	National Tournament at
24-140	24-166	24-192	72-498	White Sulphur Springs.
			———	August, 1896.
			144-990	
24-134	24-148	24-190	72-472	Norwood, Ohio, Sept.
24-156	24-168	24-184	72-508	29th, 1898.
			———	
			144-980	

46-272 National Tournament. Ludlow Grove, Cincinnati,
48-316 Ohio, July 12th, 1883.
48-352
———
142-940

Single Columbia Round

23-147   Practice at Wyoming, Ohio, August 31st, 1883.
24-180
24-182
———
71-509

24-138   Practice. August 10th, 1895.
24-176
24-194
———
72-508

24-166   Practice. July 28th, 1883.
23-163
24-176
———
71-505

22-144   National Tournament. Dayton, Ohio, August 21st,
24-178   1895.
24-182
———
70-504

(Editor's Note: It is obvious that one or both of the single rounds making up the Double Columbia Round of 1048 must have been greater than the scores here given.)

Single American Round
- 28–174   Practice. July 25th, 1883.
- 30–190
- 30–210
- 88–574

Ladies' Team Round (96 arrows at 50 yards)
- 24–146   National Tournament, White Sulphur Springs,
- 24–168   August 20th, 1896.
- 24–138
- 24–180
- 96–632

- 23–129   Also made at the National Tournament at White
- 24–140   Sulphur Springs, 1896.
- 24–138
- 23–115
- 94–522

(96 arrows at 40 yards)
- 24–150   National Tournament, Dayton, August 23rd, 1895.
- 24–158
- 24–164
- 24–160
- 96–632

"I allowed myself *no* practice arrows, before beginning my scoring."

Best Scores of All Kinds 131

MISS CYNTHIA M. WESSON, *Cotuit, Mass.*
(*Sometimes of Bryn Mawr, Pa.*)

Writing under date of May 9th, 1916, Miss Wesson gives her best practice scores as follows:

Single National Round
    48–314   July 17th, 1915. 24 golds.
    23–171
    ―――
    71–485

Single Columbia Round
    24–170   July 18th, 1915. 37 golds.
    24–182
    24–208
    ―――
    72–560

Single American Round
    30–186   July 21st, 1915. 27 golds.
    30–186
    30–222
    ―――
    90–594

MISS MARY WILLIAMS, *Chicago, Ill.*

On June 11th, 1910, in a club contest of the Chicago Archery Association, when only 12 years of age, Miss Williams shot a Single National Round, which made a record, so far as we know, for so young an archer.

    60   50   Total
  20–110
  23–141
  ―――
  43–251 22–130 65–381

While the foregoing scores show the best performances at the targets and ordinary ranges, there are many other feats of skill that are of interest. A succession of good scores are evidence of sustained power, even though none of them be the best the archer has ever made, excellent shooting may be done at irregular marks, or prowess in hunting game with the bow and arrow may demand recognition.

Such deeds will be mentioned at random, under the names of the individuals who accomplished them.

CAPTAIN F. S. BARNES, *Forest Grove, Oregon.*

Shot at least three deer and a mountain lion.

C. C. BEACH, *Battle Creek, Mich.*

Best 30 arrows at 60 yards	30-198
" 30 " " 50 "	30-216
" 30 " " 40 "	30-242
Hypothetical round	90-656

GEORGE PHILLIPS BRYANT, *Melrose, Mass.*

In answer to a letter asking for his best scores, Mr. Bryant said: "I enclose a record of what I consider the best shooting I ever did. York Rounds shot consecutively, July, 1912.

100 yards	80 yards	60 yards	Total
56–246	45–251	24–152	125–649
56–216	44–246	24–150	124–612
52–206	45–255	24–152	121–613
55–225	48–284	24–128	127–637
57–269	47–235	24–142	128–646
61–293	45–251	24–158	130–702

My bow broke in the last end of the last York, which settled this run of scores."

Mr. Gray, who saw all of these splendid York Rounds shot, said to the writer that the arrows seemed to fly down the range as though they were all tied to one invisible wire.

Best 24 arrows at 60 yards	23–167
" 30 " " 60 "	30–206
" 30 " " 50 "	30–224
" 30 " " 40 "	30–238
Hypothetical round	90–668

FRANK E. CANFIELD, *Chicago*.

In a letter to the writer, December, 1910, Dr. E. B. Weston says, "I once saw my friend Canfield shoot a little over 300 yards, using a 56 pound lemonwood bow and flight arrows of his own make.

DR. E. I. COLE, *Ossining, New York*.

30 arrows at 20 yards	
999999	6– 54
999999	6– 54
799999	6– 52
999997	6– 52
999977	6– 50
	30–262

W. J. Compton, *Portland, Oregon.*

In a letter dated November 5th, 1916, Dr. Saxton Pope gives the following account of this remarkable man. He is a professional hunter who uses a bow because he thinks it is more sportsmanlike than using a rifle.

"Compton wrote out for me just what game he has killed, as nearly as he can remember. He began shooting the bow at 14 years, in 1877, in Nebraska at the head of the Elkhorn River. The Sioux Indians were his teachers. He uses the Sioux release, a tertiary type, all the fingers on the string, below the nock, thumb lightly touching nock, a very powerful loose.

He killed his first deer with a bow in September, 1877, shooting it in a "blow-out" at 10 yards distance, through the heart.

Later in the same year he killed a fawn, with three arrows and much chasing.

During the next few years he killed about 20 deer in this country, within a radius of 100 miles. Also four antelope, one cow elk three years old and one yearling.

In 1880 he shot a buffalo, a two year old. He hit him about the middle but did not finish him, the Indians did this with guns.

This was between Crow Creek and the Little Missouri, almost the last stand of the bison.

In Wyoming, in 1883, he killed a big buck antelope by severing his spinal cord with an arrow at about 50 yards.

In Big Horn Mountains, in 1884, he shot, but failed to kill outright, a black bear, chasing him for almost an hour. In this place he also shot a big buck through the heart at 82 paces. He also made another heart shot at 50 yards.

In the Cascade Mountains of Oregon he killed a mountain beaver, a very rare animal, never known to be shot with a gun.

Besides these he has killed several hundred rabbits, many quail, a few ducks on the wing, sage hens, prairie chickens, doves, grouse, a few squirrels, chipmunks, groundhogs, two skunks so dead they had no time to register a complaint, four coons, two badgers and some tame cats.

I have seen him kill dozens of rabbits, small birds, wound two deer and kill another, using broad heads and a 65 pound bow. He can shoot an 80 pound bow.

The best shot I ever saw, Compton made at this deer. We started him and, as he bounded down a very steep hill side, at about 65 yards, Compton let drive. The deer was running quartering away from us. Just as it swerved slightly to enter the brush, say at 75 yards, the arrow connected with him. Compton released at 65 and hit the deer, which was not going at full speed, at about 75 yards. It caught him in the short ribs on the right side, and ranged forward, making an exit back of the opposite shoulder, sticking out a foot. The deer dashed into the undergrowth, some small bak or laurel bushes. As it did so it snapped off the arrow shaft, leaving only the feathers visible in the side. Compton went and picked up the shaft. On its point were blood, green food and lung tissue. We knew we had him. About an hour later we found him huddled up against some small madrone trees, 200 yards down the canyon, dead. A good sized forked horn. Our autopsy showed that the arrow had penetrated the stomach, diaphragm, lung and base of heart. The pericardial and pleural cavities were flooded with blood.

This was a beautiful shot, good luck, good archery, and good judgment of distance."

Arthur Young
Shoots fish in California

Dr. Saxton Pope
and first buck for 1917

W. J. Compton and Arthur Young. A bird apiece

Dr. Saxton Pope
and his composite bow

Best Scores of All Kinds

MRS. JOHN DUNLAP, JR., *Wayne, Pa.*

On November 29th, 1913, shooting the 100 yard distance of the last York in the N. A. A. Mail Match, she made an end of 99773 5-35, probably a record for a woman.

DR. ROBERT P. ELMER, *Wayne, Pa.*

In 1915, shooting the American Round twice a week or oftener till after the National Tournament, had every score above 500.

In September, 1917, shot eight consecutive American Rounds, in private practice, as follows:

September	6	30–180	30–214	30–222	90–616
"	7	29–187	30–224	30–216	89–627
"	11	30–196	30–208	30–224	90–628
"	11	30–196	30–222	30–216	90–634
"	14	30–200	30–218	30–218	90–636
"	17	29–191	30–222	30–242	89–655
"	18	30–194	30–200	30–242	90–636
"	19	30–196	30–194	30–222	90–612

The above rounds were made with a yew-backed yew by Barnes, 1911, five feet ten inches long and weighing 48 pounds, and McChesney's arrows, 403 grains.

Best 30 arrows at 60 yards	30–200	Sept. 14 as above.
" 30 " " 50 "	30–224	Sept. 11 as above.
" 30 " " 40 "	30–242	Sept. 17 and 18 as above, and at Chicago August 7, 1915.
Hypothetical round	90–666	

Aug. 7th, 1915	6- 46	Sept. 17th, 1917	6- 46	Sept. 18th, 1917	6- 54
	6- 46		6- 50		6- 48
17 golds	6- 46		6- 50	19 golds	6- 46
12 reds	6- 52		6- 48	8 reds	6- 42
1 blue	6- 52		6- 48	3 blues	6- 52
	30-242		30-242		30-242

The first ten arrows at 40 yards on Sept. 18th were golds. Made 11 successive golds at 40 yards, being the last arrow of the first end, all of the second end and the first five of the third end, in a match at the Cynwyd Club, May, 1915. Scored by Esther M. Weyl. 6-46, 6-54, 6-50, 6-46, 6-44, 30-240. 18 golds in all. Made with Duff's arrows.

Best American Round shot in a match was made 17th September, 1916, at the Cynwyd Club, Cynwyd, Pa., and scored by Dr. E. F. Corson.

30-196 30-216 30-228 90-640   In this round a Barnes' self yew (6 feet, 42 pounds) was used with Duff's arrows (409 grains).

FRANK C. HAVENS, *Oakland, California.*

Best 30 arrows at 60 yards   30-202
"   30 "   " 50   "   30-212
"   30 "   " 40   "   30-246   (18 golds, 12 reds.)

Hypothetical score   90-660

DR. OWEN L. HERTIG, *Pittsburgh, Pa.*

This extract from a letter to the writer, dated March 20th, 1912, is well worth preserving:

"As a boy, from the age of twelve until I started to college, I was, after a fashion, a skillful archer. Shooting home made weapons, unfeathered hickory arrows, tipped with Norway iron points, using primary loose, and placing arrow on right hand side of bow, I was able at short range, to do some very creditable and, I may say, remarkable work. Here are a few samples which my memory holds clearly and distinctly:

Placing 10 consecutive arrows in old-fashioned oyster can at 20 yards, that is, hitting a space 4 by 6 inches.

Shooting through an inch auger hole at 18 feet 35 times straight.

Hitting a pie pan thrown into the air 100 times straight at 20 feet.

Hitting consistently any object thrown into the air, no matter how small.

Placing, at 10 yards, 95% of arrows in a four inch circle.

At 20 feet shooting tin box lid 3 inches in diameter, from hand of boy companion and pinning it to the wall. This last feat I did repeatedly until my father caught me at it. The boy, A. H. Sayers, now a prominent attorney of my old home Waynesbury, Pa., was the instigator of the thing for which I was punished."

The best practice shooting he has done with regular methods and equipment was in October and November, 1913, when, in 54 consecutive rounds, 24 York, 18 American, and 12 Team he averaged in the York 113-517, in the American 88-532 and in the Team 93-527. In that fall he won the York Round in the series of 10 mail matches conducted by the N.A.A., in a field of 24. He shot in 8 matches with a low score 106-484, high 122-596 and average 114-535. In sending his last mail match score, in November, he wrote, "I have dropped only three arrows out of 350 at 60 yards. In the old English round of 144 arrows at 60 yards I made 143-867. The English record is 142-840, made by the Rev. Rimington."

Z. E. JACKSON, *Atchison, Kansas*. He has done a great deal of hunting, especially of small animals and birds. While seated in a canoe, in 1911, on a lake in British Columbia, he shot and killed a deer at 60 yards distance, the arrow passing through both shoulders an inch in front of the heart. (Thompson, *Forest & Stream*, March, 1915.)

Best Scores of All Kinds

Louis W. Maxson, *Washington, D. C.* (*Deceased.*)

At Washington Grove, Maryland, on July 11th, 1890, before a large number of spectators, Mr. Maxson shot three exhibition rounds without stopping, which, as a whole, have never been beaten.

	1st	2nd	3rd
60	30–186	30–204	30–210
50	30–202	30–210	30–216
40	30–242	30–234	30–240
	90–630	90–648	90–666

Euclid D. Miller, *Tennessee.*

Besides having killed "most every kind of game in this country," (see *Forest & Stream*, October 25th, 1913), he adopted the Y-shaped pile from the Japanese and used it to decapitate snakes.

F. E. Perry, *Battle Creek, Michigan.*

30 arrows at 30 yards   30–260, with 16 successive golds.

Dr. Saxton T. Pope, *San Francisco, Cal.*

> "Strong of arm was Hiawatha;
> He could shoot ten arrows upward,
> Shoot them with such strength and swiftness,
> That the tenth had left the bow-string
> Ere the first to earth had fallen."
> (Hiawatha and Mudjekeewis, Lines 11–15.)

In the past it has been supposed by archers who have tried to accomplish this feat that it was possible only in the imagination of the poet. In recent times, however, Dr. Pope seems to have brought it so near fulfillment that it is no longer scoffed at. In a letter dated November 5th, 1916, he writes:

"I made up seven shafts with V-nocks and grooved so I could catch them quickly and feel the right side. Then I practiced 15 minutes every day for one week; just nocking and releasing. Today I tried myself out and three times in succession I kept seven arrows in the air at once. Even with this I had time to fumble one or two and still had sixty feet leeway on the last arrow. With diligence I could easily shoot eight arrows. The first arrow I used was a flight arrow. It required eight seconds to complete its course, almost perpendicular."

As other archers have been able to keep only three arrows in the air at once, Pope's explanation of his method will interest them.

"By holding the arrows on the right side of the bow, drawing one after another over the thumb, using a release of my own invention, where the thumb and first finger grasp the arrow yet stay on the right of the string, assisted by the other fingers, and shooting

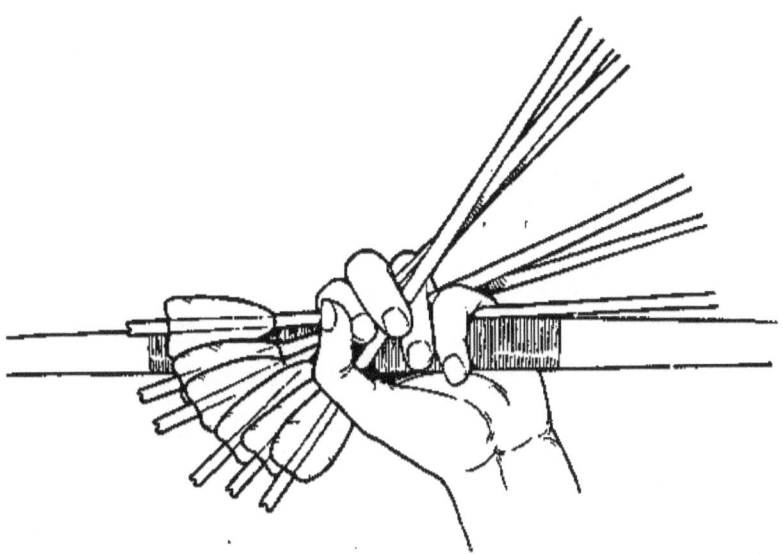

Dr. Pope's left hand, in keeping seven arrows in the air at once.

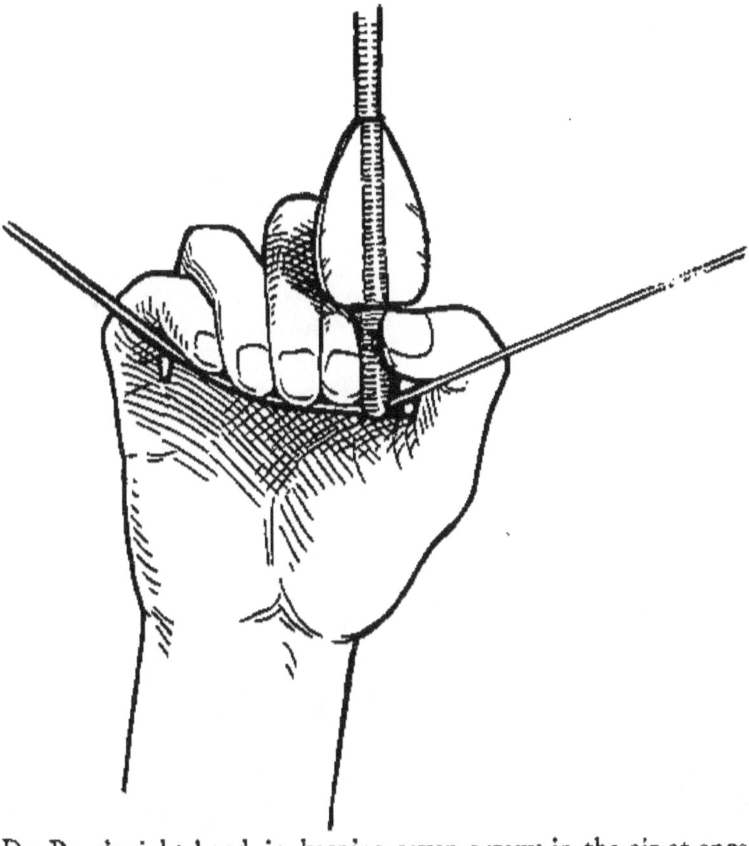

Dr. Pope's right hand, in keeping seven arrows in the air at once.

the first arrow as usual, I get away with this feat of dexterity, if not utility."

If any man can equal Hiawatha it ought to be Pope, as he is a prestidigitator of the greatest skill, wonderfully quick of hand.

The following quotation from an article called "What a Good Bow Has Done and Will Do," by Will H. Thompson, in *Forest & Stream* for March, 1915, gives an idea of the difficulty of Pope's accomplishment. Mr. Thompson is the dean of American archers and, as he says himself, speaks *ex cathedra*.

"No man of any age, race, time or with a record for previous condition of servitude, ever could perform or ever has performed the feat of shooting 'so far and so fast as to have six arrows in the air at once.' Seriously, after more than fifty years of the bow, and much experimentation, I have never been able to keep three arrows in the air at one time but have come so near it that I feel sure it might be done. I feel equally sure that no man ever has, ever will, or now can, keep four in the air at one time. A very slight increase of speed might be secured by having large open nocks in the arrows, so that one could quickly *feel* the arrow on to the string, but the gain would not be sufficient to get an additional arrow (over three) into the air."

Under the tutelage of Ishi and Compton, Dr. Pope has become a very good hunter, having killed a deer and a great many small animals.

PROFESSOR E. J. RENDTORFF, *Lake Forest, Illinois.*

Without doubt Prof. Rendtorff is one of the greatest archers the world has ever seen He is the only American in the class of Horace Ford. On his private range and on the grounds of the Chicago Archery Association his shooting has been witnessed by a great many people who were thoroughly qualified to pass judgment and they unanimously say that his skill is fully as great as his published scores would indicate. Unfortunately he has been able to appear in only one open contest, the Pre-Olympic Carnival at Grant Park, Chicago, July 3rd, 4th and 5th, 1913. On that occasion the wind was so high that it blew up blinding clouds of dust and the targets had to be firmly moored with guy ropes. Under such conditions his scores, which were recorded by

Best Scores of All Kinds 145

Homer S. Taylor, are remarkable. They are:

Double York

42–146	45–233	23–141	110–520
37–149	40–196	22–124	99–469
			209–989

Double American

29–169	30–212	30–218	89– 599
30–160	30–194	30–216	90– 570
			179–1169

Team

24–148	24–140	22–130	24–144	94–562

The score by ends of his record breaking American Round are of interest to everybody. They are:

60 yards	50 yards	40 yards	
6– 44	6– 46	6– 46	
6– 44	6– 50	6– 48	
6– 44	6– 40	6– 50	
6– 46	6– 40	6– 44	
6– 46	6– 52	6– 42	
30–224	30–228	30–230	90–682

In a letter to *Forest & Stream* he says: "I had distinctly seen no point of aim at 60 yards, but judged its location subconsciously. At 50 yards a small space of bare ground helped me, while at 40 yards a darker patch of grass proved of assistance. In every case I had my direct vision on the gold and the indirect or secondary vision on the point of aim, which I need for elevation purposes only and not for lateral alignment."

DR. HENRY B. RICHARDSON, *Boston, Mass.*

Dr. Richardson is the only American archer, of any consequence, who has ever competed in the great matches of England. It is therefore gratifying to his countrymen to know that he not only held his own, in every event, with the best of his opponents but even, in the one match whose records went back almost to the time when archery was the national sport,—namely, the Scorton Arrow contest which began in 1673,—made the best score ever recorded.

He went abroad in the summer of 1908, at the age of 19, while he was champion of the United States. The following records of his performances were taken from "The Field," by Dr. Weston.

		Single York Round		
Royal Toxophilite Society Regent's Park, July 9th				
H. B. Richardson	34–150	36–148	23–121	93–419
H. P. Nesham	31–197	26– 88	22–112	79–397
Olympic Games, July 17–18				
W. Dod	70–292	71–299	44–224	185–815
Brooks-King	68–250	72–300	44–218	184–768
Richardson	60–248	67–291	43–221	170–760

On the third day of the tournament a handicap York was shot in which Richardson, who was scratch, made the highest mark of

105–453. Dod won the match with 82 given, his net being 99–453.

Grand National. Trinity College Cricket Ground, Oxford, July 22, 23 and 24

Double York Round

Richardson	88–362	75–335	38–174	201–871
Brooks-King	77–319	72–342	43–209	192–870

Dod, who won the Olympic Games, was seventh.

After the shooting was all over and everybody thought Richardson had won, an old rule was dug up which said that the championship could be won only by a native of the British Isles. The match was therefore given to Brooks-King.

Antient Scorton Arrow. 235th Annual Competition. July 29th.

This competition is at 100 yards, two arrows being shot at an end. No specified number of arrows are shot, but the shooting takes two hours in the morning and two in the afternoon. At this meeting 178 arrows were shot.

The Field says: "Mr. Richardson shot in great form, and made the highest score, in hits and score, that has ever been recorded."

Richardson	162–452	Golds 9
C. H. Coates	61–269	" 5
T. T. S. Metcalfe	50–198	" 4

Grand-Western. Sherbourne, August 12, 13 and 14.
  Double York Round
    Brooks-King   190-824
    T. Robinson   168-740
    Richardson   151-655
Mid-Herefordshire Archery Society. August 18th.
  (96 arrows at 80 yards and 48 at 60 yards)
    Ingham   72-358
    Backhouse   78-357
    Richardson   60-276
Herefordshire York Round Club. August 19th.
  Single York Round
    Richardson   77-359
    Backhouse   72-334
Grand Northern. August 26, 27 and 28.
  Double York Round
    Keysworth   161-639
    Hussey   158-628
    Richardson   149-611

HOMER S. TAYLOR, *Greenfield, Mass. Until lately of Chicago.*

Mr. Taylor was present at the first National Tournament in 1879, though only as a spectator. The next year he began competitive shooting and from then till the present time, with a lapse of a few years in the late '80s, he has always been one of the best shots in the country. Before the National Tournament last year (1916) he had had almost no practice yet he won third place. The longer the shooting lasted the better he got. On the last day, shooting at a life sized silhouette of a duck at 40 yards he put five arrows out of six in a space the size of a man's hand. It is an inspiration to every archer to see a man who is no longer young doing such splendid work.

From among many excellent performances the following twelve York Rounds, shot in succession, may be taken as a sample of his steadiness, although in 1911 his scores, which are not at hand, were probably even better.

1908	100 yards	80 yards	60 yards	Total
Aug. 21	46–216	38–190	24–152	108–558
Aug. 28	53–225	43–191	24–136	120–552
Aug. 29	52–212	40–174	24–128	116–514
Sept. 7	51–235	41–185	22–116	114–536
Sept. 7	39–137	42–196	23–127	104–460
Sept. 20	49–213	40–226	22–120	111–559
Sept. 26	50–220	40–220	21–111	111–551
Sept. 27	39–165	35–167	22– 92	96–424
Oct. 3	52–228	41–207	21–115	114–550
Oct. 4	49–207	44–204	23–119	116–530
Oct. 4	53–207	43–209	22– 86	118–502

MUARICE THOMPSON, *Crawfordsville, Indiana.* (*Deceased.*)

Best 24 arrows at 60 yards   24–176
"   30   "   " 60 "   30–216
"   30   "   " 40 "   30–244   (18 golds, 11 reds, 1 blue)

In October, 1878, he broke 35 out of 50 glass balls thrown into the air at 10 yards. (Reported in *Chicago Field* of that month.)

He killed innumerable birds and animals, as related in "*The Witchery of Archery*" an many other writings. Every archer should read his stories.

WILL H. THOMPSON, *Seattle, Washington.*

Brother of Maurice Thompson and his companion on his hunting trips. Killed all kinds of birds and animals. Both men were invincible in off-hand shooting.

Best 30 arrows at 60 yards	30–198	
" 30 " " 50 "	30–204	
" 30 " " 40 "	30–236	
	90–638	
Best 30 arrows at 20 yards	30–268	(29 golds, 1 red)

COLONEL ROBERT WILLIAMS, *Washington, D. C. (Deceased.)*

Up to 1888 had made 13 Double York Rounds of over 1000. Eleven were in 1883.

ARTHUR YOUNG, *San Francisco.*

Pope wrote: "Young killed 17 ground squirrels in one afternoon with the bow, at distances of from 10 to 40 yards. Five of these he killed with five successive arrows."

"He shot 15 carp, one morning, in a backwater of the Tuolumne River, a feat not known to have been equalled by a white man."

TEAMS

In the Ohio State Archery Association's Annual Tournament in 1883, the Men's

Team of the Highland Archers, of Wyoming, Ohio, made the highest score ever recorded in this country.

90 arrows at 60 yards

A. W. Houston	94– 604
W. A. Clark	95– 597
H. W. Pollock	88– 478
C. S. Woodruff	82– 444
	359–2123

A very good practice score was made by the Pittsburgh Archers in May, 1914.

Holmes	92– 528
Sorber	91– 505
Hertig	91– 457
Jiles	89– 423
	363–1913

It is a pity that they did not make one point more to commemorate the year!

The following is translated from "Le Tir a l'Arc;" "Finally, we mention for the sceptics who deny the possibility of shooting on the wing with the bow, that Maurice Thompson made the American record for it in 1894. He has, in fact, in a public tournament, broken 38 glass balls, and in a private match 48, out of 50 thrown into the air at a distance of about 12 metres."

CHAPTER XIII

THE REDDENDO ARROWS

By J. Mark Mauser

IN 1914 Mr. James Duff, of the Scottish-American Archers of Jersey City, made a trophy to be competed for by the various archery clubs, with the idea of bringing them into more frequent contact. It consists of a pair of arrows, beautifully inlaid with ebony, feathered with the finest of white goose feathers, tipped with barbed bronze points and laid parallel upon a finely polished oak board.

These handsome shafts are copied from the arrows which the Royal Company of Archers, the King's bodyguard for Scotland, present to the monarch on his formal visits to that country, a feu-duty, or "Reddendo," by virtue of which they have held their charter since 1703.

Duff's "Reddendo Arrows" are shot for under the following conditions:

> A challenge must be given at least thirty days before the match. The match may be the American Round, the Team Round or the York Round, but the round selected must be agreeable to both, or all, sides.

The Reddendo Arrows

There is no maximum limit to the number of archers on a team, but not less than four may compete. One team may contain more archers than the other; in which case the best scores of the larger side shall be counted, equal to the number of those of the smaller team.

The first challenge was sent by the Scottish-American Archers to the Wayne Archers, the match taking place at Jersey City on June 20th, 1914, with the following scores:

Wayne Archers		Scottish-American Archers	
Dr. R. P. Elmer	90– 530	R. McNeil	69– 323
J. M. Mauser	77– 405	F. N. Clay	58– 306
A. C. Hale	70– 376	J. McCrae	59– 283
G. W. Watt	47– 229	J. Duff	61– 269
E. E. Trout	42– 212	G. Milne	56– 256
C. L. Lehman	49– 181	J. Cleland	60– 244
	375–1933		363–1681

A challenge from the newly formed Walden Archers, of the Lehigh Valley, was almost immediately sent to the Wayne club and accepted, with this result:

August 1st, 1914
Wayne, Pa.

Wayne Archers		Walden Archers	
Dr. Elmer	90– 560	J. M. Mauser	90– 522
T. T. Hare	87– 453	J. M. Ramsey	51– 233
A. C. Hale	66– 304	H. J. Lentz	37– 183
E. E. Trout	45– 211	Rutter	27– 105
	288–1528		205–1043

The Walden Archers, although defeated, continued to put in a lot of practice and again challenged the Wayne club, this time with more success.

Sept. 26th, 1914
  Laurys Station, Pa.

Walden Archers			Wayne Archers		
J. M. Mauser	85–	485	Dr. Elmer	86–	516
G. Mauser	86–	474	A. C. Hale	65–	341
J. M. Ramsey	65–	295	E. E. Trout	58–	264
H. J. Lerch	66–	294	C. L. Lehman	45–	169
	302–	1548		254–	1290

The next match, on a challenge from Wayne, ended the season.

Oct. 24th, 1914
  Wayne

Walden Archers			Wayne Archers		
J. M. Mauser	86–	500	Dr. Elmer	90–	584
G. Mauser	86–	436	E. E. Trout	75–	369
H. J. Lerch	73–	293	A. C. Hale	73–	347
H. J. Lentz	66–	290	F. L. Bodine	57–	253
J. M. Ramsey	57–	259	C. L. Lehman	44–	156
	348–	1778		339–	1709

Next year the Jersey Scotchmen issued a challenge to the Walden Archers and once again the Lehigh men were victorious.

Oct. 23rd, 1915
Jersey City

Walden Archers		Scottish-Americans	
H. J. Lentz	84– 480	J. Duff	80– 408
J. M. Mauser	82– 422	J. McCrae	77– 385
H. J. Lerch	80– 366	G. Milne	72– 340
G. Mauser	68– 322	Rev. E. I. Cole	67– 321
	314–1590		296–1454

In 1916 the Jersey club turned the tables on the Walden Archers in a match held at Sheepshead Bay, N. Y., in connection with the Open Championship Archery Tournament.

May 24th, 1916
Sheepshead Bay, N. Y.

Scottish-Americans		Walden Archers	
J. Duff	79– 413	J. M. Mauser	86– 484
J. M. Cleland	60– 316	H. J. Lerch	63– 281
J. McCrae	63– 309	H. J. Lentz	62– 240
G. Milne	66– 306	G. Mauser	43– 143
	238–1344		254–1178

This trophy has added much to the interest in archery in the Middle Eastern States, for instance the idea of winning it was the direct means of creating the well known Walden Archers, of Laurys Station. As a rule a match has formed a nucleus for a much larger contest at the same time, many other archers, both men and women, participating in the shooting and sociability. It is to be hoped that challenges will soon be issued by Boston, Chicago, Pittsburgh and other clubs.

CHAPTER XIV

Scoring by "Points"

By Dr. Robert P. Elmer

ARCHERS of the future may wonder what is meant when they read, in a list of winners, the expression, "A had the best score but B won on *points*."

The fact is that when the National Archery Association was organized it was thought best to conform the methods of shooting and scoring with those in use in England, partly for the reason that the English were supposed to have found out from experience what the best things were and partly so that it would be more easy to compare the performances of the archers on both sides of the ocean.

For some unknown reason the English were in the habit of keeping what might be called a score of the score. In other words, after adding up the actual values of the hits they gave to the figures a secondary or arbitrary value by awarding "points" on a purely factitious basis and thereby deciding the outcome of the match. The specific meaning of this can be understood by studying the following tables, which show how the "points" for the different events, were awarded.

York Round				National Round			
Greatest Total Score		2	points	Greatest Total Score		2	points
"	" Hits	2	"	"	" Hits	2	"
"	100 yard Score	1	point	"	60 yard Score	1	point
"	" " Hits	1	"	"	" " Hits	1	"
"	80 " Score	1	"	"	50 " Score	1	"
"	" " Hits	1	"	"	" " Hits	1	"
"	60 " Score	1	"				
"	" " Hits	1	"				
		10				8	

The American and Columbia Rounds were decided in a similar manner.

The second National Tournament, at Buffalo, was awarded on score, not on points, but in the following year the authorities decided to use the point system again and then for thirty years it remained, to be a bone of contention and a source of ill feeling at many a tournament.

The unfairness of the method lay in the fact that it permitted an outsider to step in and rob the man who had done the best shooting of some of his points. While a great number of cases might be cited we will take one that occurred in the Eastern Archery Association in 1914 and which may be found on page 7. Or again, in the National Tournament of 1913 G. P. Bryant was nosed out of first place by Dr. J. W. Doughty in the following manner:

	Bryant			Doughty		
Total Score	832	2	points	802	0	points
Total Hits	176	0	"	178	2	"
Score at 100	279	0	"	282	1	"
Hits at 100	65	0	"	66	1	point
Score at 80	315	1	point	254	0	"
Hits at 80	67	1	"	66	0	"
Score at 60	238	0	"	266	1	"
Hits at 60	44	0	"	46	0	"
		4			6	

This example is not like that taken from the Eastern A. A. because here no third party intervened. Still, the fact remained that the man whose arrows had totalled up the highest figure did not win the match.

The only good argument for the point system was that at the 100 yard range it required skill to hit the target at all, for instance eight hits in the white, out of eight arrows, would show more skill than one hit in the gold with seven misses, and that the point system, by giving credit for the number of hits, recognized that fact. As this reasoning could not be held by anyone to apply to the American and Columbia Rounds the point system was abolished for them in 1913, two years before it was done away with altogether. It was not till 1915 that the opinion became universal that the system was cumbersome, archaic and disagreeable. When the new constitution was adopted at the Annual Business Meeting of that year the opportunity was taken to adopt the present method which certainly seems, in its practical working, to be the simplest and best.

CHAPTER XV

FLIGHT SHOOTING

By Dr. Robert P. Elmer

TO THOSE who do not object to walking, no branch of archery is more fascinating than flight-shooting. There is an exhilaration about it which is due partly to the greater physical effort required and partly to the esthetic enjoyment of the free flight of the shaft, which looks as though it would pierce the very clouds. Those archers who make their own tackle are apt to practice flight-shooting, because the problems arising in connection with it are almost impossible to solve and afford unending opportunity for experimentation in manufacturing flight bows and flight arrows. Few men are agreed on what is the best equipment, for instance one will claim that long arrows are the best, while another will argue for short ones and yet, when put to the practical test of shooting, both will get good results. We can only tell what our experience has found to be of value, hoping that others will continue to

Flight Shooting

get pleasure and profit by trying out their original ideas.

Bows

The shorter the bow the farther it will cast. This is because a short bow will resume its original shape more quickly from a full draw than will a long weapon. The only reason for bows being as long as they usually are is the prevention of breaking. The Turkish and Persian bows are only about 30 inches long but they will shoot farther than any other bows in the world. In June, 1913, Ingo Simon, an Englishman, at Le Touquet, France, shot 459 yards and 8 inches with a Turkish bow said to be 200 years old. Still longer shots are probably authentic. In 1795, Mahmoud Effendi, Secretary of the Turkish Embassy at London, sent home for a bow, in order to show the superiority of the weapons of his country over those of England, and, in a carefully witnessed trial, made a shot of 482 yards.

The Turkish bows can be so short because they are not made of wood only, but are composite bows with a belly of horn and a back of sinew laid on a thin, flat piece of wood which forms a central core.

The fact that short bows of the English pattern will cast far is borne out by experience. For instance, Mr. Duff made a bow, in 1910, of lemonwood back and washaba belly, which was only five feet long and weighed 87 pounds for a 21 inch draw. Three trial shots gave 241½ yards for the first two arrows, which landed together, and 276 yards 9 inches for the third. Mr. Duff was certain that the bow was good for many yards more than this, if he could have practiced with it but, on the fourth draw, the lemonwood back pulled apart, breaking the bow. If the back had been hickory, with its much greater tensile strength, the catastrophe might not have occurred. It seems probable that if one could so combine his materials as to make a five foot bow, with hickory back and hard wood belly, drawing 90 pounds for 21 inches and able to stand a still further draw to 25 inches, he would have a weapon that would do all that could be expected of a bow of the English type. For such a bow small blocks glued to the belly and nocked for the string are better than horns.

Although the bow just described represents the choice of the writer, it must be stated

Flight Shooting 163

that the majority of authorities flatly deny that the use of such a strong weapon is advisable. In support of their view many cases like the following can be cited.

Horace Ford made his best shot of 308 yards with a 68 pound yew.

Mr. Muir, of Edinburgh, although a very skillful archer and a man of great strength, found that he could shoot farther with a 60 pound bow than with a heavier one.

Mr. Troward, of England, in 1798, made 340 yards up and down wind with a self-bow pulling 63 pounds and 29 inch flight arrows. The bows used in all of these shots were presumably six feet long.

On the other hand Sir Ralph P. Galway, in 1905, in the presence of James Duff, shot 376 yards with a Turkish bow weighing 100 pounds and the bow used by Ingo Simon in his record breaking shot weighed 80 pounds.

Reflexion adds to the cast of a bow. The Turkish bows are reflexed to such an extreme degree that, when unstrung, they vary in form from a curve like the letter C to the shape of a pretzel. The only Turkish bows known to be in this country are in museums and there one usually sees them with the string put on while they are still unbent. This is because it seems incredible to the curators that they could possibly be bent around as far as they should be in order to be strung, even though the situation of the nocks would clearly indicate such a fact to an archer. Such very great reflexion is only possible in a bow that is made of much more elastic materials than wood alone, and also in a bow that is broad and flat, because a half round bow, like those of the English would have a strong tendency to side twist if drawn out of line. However, a long bow reflected to a moderate angle is somewhat quickened thereby, because the fibres of the wood are already in a state of greater tension, and therefore greater resiliency, before the draw is begun.

Arrows

The success of a flight shot depends more on the arrow than on the bow.

The Turks use a 21 inch arrow which is drawn back to 25 inches. This extra distance is made possible by the use of a bone guide fastened to the wrist, so that the arrow can be drawn behind the bow. A similar contrivance is necessary for the short bow which the writer has advocated above, if a short arrow is to be used for a long draw. It is objected that if the idea of a short shaft and long guide were carried to its logical extreme the result would be a crossbow. This, however, is only a theoretical objection, for experimentation will soon convince one that there is a practical limit in dimensions beyond which it is not advantageous to go, and that this limit is placed where the essential features of long bow shooting are in no sense lost. Ingo Simon and Sir Ralph Galway used guides fastened to the wrist in the Turkish fashion. The writer uses one made of bone 1½ inches wide and 6 inches long, which is wired to the bow at the arrowplate.

The arrow with which the writer won the Flight Shoot at the National Tournament in 1911 was an ordinary Whitman target arrow, weighing about 300 grains, with the feathers cut down to mere nubbins. The bow was a 65 pound lemonwood, 5 feet 8 inches long, fitted with the guide just mentioned. On that occasion Mr. Homer Bishop had three barrelled flight arrows, one of which was made hollow, to obtain light weight with stiffness. They were tried by the writer with the same bow but would not fly nearly so far, possibly because they had the ordinary balloon feathers of target arrows.

The arrows with which Mr. and Mrs. Bryant, Mrs. Frentz and Mr. Jiles have won the flight shoot in recent years have all been similar. They have been about 28 or 29 inches long, weighing about 250 grains, somewhat barrelled, except in the case of bamboo, in order to have enough spine, with the center of gravity near the center of the shaft, with a small steel pile and with two little feathers about ¾ inch long and ¼ inch high. Mrs. Frentz's was scraped down from a Japanese arrow of reed. The others were bamboo or footed spruce.

Three flight arrows that Aldred, of England, made for the writer were 29 inches over all, weighed 298 grains, were barrelled and footed with lance. The greatest diameter was exactly $\frac{5}{16}$ inch. The piles were $\frac{3}{16}$ x ⅛ inch. There were three triangular feathers, each 2⅝ inches long and $\frac{7}{16}$ inch high. When one of these was scraped down to 260 grains it still seemed to be stiff enough but it would not fly as far as it had before, nor as far as its unaltered fellows. In fact it is not always the lightest arrow that flies farthest, even though it have a good spine. The only sure test is in the shooting.

A very important influence on the carry of a flight arrow is exerted by the feathers. When one considers that the chief obstacle to a speeding arrow is the resistance of the air, it is obvious that the feathers should offer as little surface as is compatible with the maintenance of a straight flight. As has been said, American archers use two very tiny vanes. Aldred favors three trimmed turkey feathers of the dimensions given above. The ancient Turkish arrows had rather soft feathers with untrimmed edges. Most authorities agree that the best vanes are drawn off of the short side of a remex from a turkey or peacock and left uncut, except for length. In all cases the feathers should be set close to the nock.

It is undoubtedly desirable that the pile should be very light but even here there is a limit. Experiment will show that the same flight arrow will often go farther with a light steel pile than without one.

Shooting

Using the same artillery, an expert flight-shooter can do more than an archer who has not practiced this specialty. Much therefore depends on technique.

An arrow will have the greatest possible trajectory when loosed from an elevation of 45 degrees. Nearly everyone is inclined to aim much lower than this and therefore, in order to become familiar with what the elevation is really like, it is well to have a friend stand beside the archer while he is practicing, and hold up a right angled triangle with the hypotenuse parallel to the shaft. This need be done only once or twice, and the triangle can be made in a minute by simply taking a square piece of paper and folding two opposite corners together.

The loose should be very snappy, even slashing, and done at the exact moment that the tip reaches the arrow plate, while the fingers are still drawing. There must be not even the suspicion of a pause before releasing.

At the instant of loosing the left hand should feel as though it were pressing the bow away from the archer as strongly as possible.

Mr. Will H. Thompson, whose great experience entitles him to a most respectful hearing, expressed his views on flight shooting in the following letter, dated September 13th, 1911. "I wish to say a few words about flight shooting. About 24 years ago I gave very great study to that matter and broke bows *by the dozen* trying to reach 300 yards, but finally failed by two yards. I passed 290 yards in still weather, shooting back and forth, with a snakewood bow backed with lance, using a barrelled 4.3 arrow, 28 inches long with two feathers about like this:

These were thin vanes from the narrow side of turkey feathers. The same bow would reach 235 yards with a 4.9 28 inch target arrow having ordinary feathers. The bow was six feet long. Of course a shorter bow will carry farther but will surely break. The Turkish horn bows are usually about 30 inches long, recurved, or 'set back,' so that a 28 inch draw gets a great deal out of them. The greatest distances made by them were made upon the same principle used by you, i. e. the bow carried a 'pipe' for a short, *very* light arrow to be drawn inside the bow. Using a 25 inch arrow weighing less than 2.6, and of rigid material, such as bamboo, with a very light head, a flight of 350 to 400 yards is attainable. But with a 5′ 10″ yew-backed yew, with a perfect flight arrow, (bamboo being the best yet found), 28 inches in length, 300 yards can be made with a 58 pound bow. I really do not believe that any ordinary man can loose a stronger bow than 58 pounds, possibly 60 pounds, so as to shoot any further. What he gains in *strength* he loses in keenness of loose. I have tried so many trained athletic archers and found *no* exception, that I am satisfied that nothing can possibly be gained by going beyond 60 pounds for any purpose. *Master* a 55 pound yew-backed yew; get a perfect 4.0 barrelled arrow of 28 inches, with only two narrow, short feathers set close to the nock, and with a rather swift (no jerk) continuous draw, *loose without stopping the draw*, the left hand hard gripping the bow, and you may command 300 yards. I could never quite do it."

CHAPTER XVI

AN AMERICAN ORIGIN FOR THE POINT OF AIM

By Dr. Robert P. Elmer

HORACE FORD has always been given credit for being the first man to use the method of shooting by what he, himself, called a "Point of Aim." In other words he is supposed to have originated the idea of trying to hit the target by sighting over the tip of the arrow at some other object, no matter what, which was so placed that it would cause the arrow thus aimed to have the proper elevation. That he really was the first person who taught that better shooting could be done in this way than by centering the gaze fixedly on the bulls-eye, is undoubted. On the other hand it seems very likely that such a simple help to aiming should have been discovered and used by various individuals who, for unknown reasons, did not leave any record behind them.

Last winter I unexpectedly obtained proof of this surmise in corresponding with Mr. Frederick Deming, of Litchfield, Connecticut, an archer who still possesses enthusiasm for our sport and practices it successfully although well advanced in years.

Knowing that they will be of interest to every American archer, I quote two letters from him which afford unquestionable evidence that he hit upon the idea of the "Point of Aim" quite independently of Ford or anyone else.

    Litchfield, Conn., Nov. 30th, 1916.
Dr. Robert P. Elmer,
 Dear Sir:
 It was a disappointment to me that I was unable to attend the Archery Meeting in Jersey City, for I had promised myself the pleasure of a talk with you on Archery. At the age of eighty-four I cannot expect to shoot much longer. However, there is *one* point which has always remained a mystery to me, probably because in early life I received no instruction or advice from an expert archer, though I *read* Ascham, Roberts, Hansard and Ford.

 The point to which I refer is this: while at *eighty* yards I can *get aim on* the four ft. target, at sixty yards or under, my arrow goes *over* the target, even if my aim is at the *lowest* edge of the target; so I have always dreaded the *short* distances. Can you kindly suggest any remedy for this?

My bow is 40 lbs., arrows about four shillings weight, although I have tried five shillings with no great success. Can it be that an exceedingly weak bow and exceedingly heavy arrows would help my sixty yard shooting?

I enclose diagram giving approximately the makeshift to which I resort to hit at sixty yards. Pardon me for troubling you in this matter but I really am anxious to know what has impeded me all my archery life in this short distance shooting.

Very truly yours,
FREDERICK DEMING.

The way I have to get on the target by placing a golf ball on the ground about fifty feet in *front* of the target is not, I suppose, legitimate archery, but it is the *only* way I have ever succeeded in "getting there."

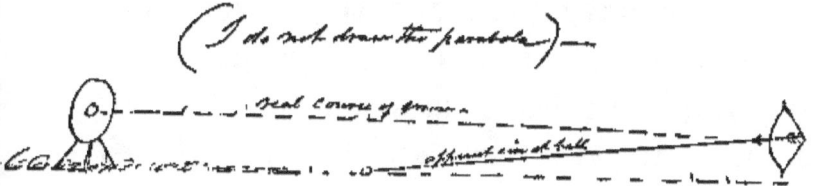

On receipt of this letter I at once wrote to him a full explanation of the "Point of Aim" and all it had meant in the development of modern archery. As an illustration I spoke of how an artillery man, by sighting with relation to some known object, could fire over the top of a mountain and hit a mark in the valley beyond.

Litchfield, Conn., Dec. 3rd, 1916.
My dear Doctor Elmer:

Your letter is a decided relief to me, for, all my archer life, I have *furtively* placed on the ground dandelion heads and the like, to get my point of aim. Twenty years before I read *Ford* I used to place a *band box* on the ground as a guide to the target, being careful to substitute something very small if there were any *spectators*. My own hard experience suggested this expedient for getting the "length." Long years afterward the following lines from Ford's book confirmed me in the belief that aiming at anything but the *target* was only a makeshift. Ford says, "One I knew, for sixty yard shooting, used actually to fix a bit of stick in the ground for that purpose;" but Ford does *not* tell *what else to do*, says it will "fail surely in matches on strange ground," etc. Now, however, I shall *mark* the "point of aim" with a *clear conscience*.

I was in the Crimea during the siege of Sebastopol in 1855. Your artillery illustration recalled to my mind the shot and shell that passed very far over our heads, from Forts Constantine and the Wasp battery. Our party, three Americans, had no business to be there, but it was just a *boys'* venture.

Thanking you for your letter throwing light on the "point of aim."

Most sincerely yours,
FREDERICK DEMING.

CHAPTER XVII

Arrowhead, the Archer's Flower

By Dr. Robert P. Elmer

AT THE Annual Business Meeting of the N. A. A. in 1914 it was voted that the Arrowhead be accepted as the official flower of archery.

The plant is an exquisitely beautiful one that grows along water courses where the current has been slowed by indentations of the bank. It owes its name to the shape of its leaves. These vary somewhat but, on the whole, bear an extraordinary resemblance to an old fashioned broad head arrow of giant size. The flower is pure white and shows well against the dark, rich green of the foliage. As a table decoration at an archery banquet nothing could be better or more appropriate than this plant.

The principal varieties of Arrowhead, or Sagittaria, are:

Sagittaria Variabilis. This is the common variety and gets its name from the fact that the leaves vary greatly in size while preserving the characteristic arrowhead form.

Sagittaria Montevidiensis (Giant Arrowhead). This attains gigantic proportions, growing 4 to 5 feet high with leaves 15 inches long. The flower scape towers above the foliage, bearing white flowers with a dark blotch at the base of each petal.

Sagittaria Japonica. Double Flowered.

Sagittaria Sinensis. The leaves are dark green, broad and strong. It grows freely and may be planted in an aquarium.

Sagittaria Natans. This is raised primarily for an aquarium plant. It has long, almost strap-like leaves, that float in the water.

CHAPTER XVIII

FRENCH AND BELGIAN ARCHERY

By Dr. Robert P. Elmer

ON SEPTEMBER 8th, 1913, the *New York Sun* printed a cable dispatch from Paris which must have caused a feeling of surprise in any native American archer who may have read it. It was as follows:

"There were 1483 competitors in the annual archery match at Noyon, in the Department of the Oise, which was completed today. It was won by Prodean, who will hence forth have the proud title of Grand Archer of France.

"The competition, which is keenly disputed by 700 clubs, has been in uninterrupted existence for 400 years. Today the archers with unerring precision split the targets with wonderful force."

Most of us have heard, all our lives, of archery as a peculiarly English sport and I, for one, confess that I was amazed when I learned that the interest in the art is very much more widespread in Belgium and North-eastern France, and the number of bowmen vastly greater there than in England.

In England it is a rich man's game, whereas on the Continent it is a pastime of the masses. A French viscount who is a member of the Wayne Archers says that he never heard of it in France although he lived in Paris, where some archery societies exist. Belgian archers whom I have talked with in Chicago said that it was a game for the workingman, in the long summer evenings after the day's task was done.

The bows they use are beautiful instruments. They are all backed, sometimes of more than two laminae, and are made of hard wood, usually of a dark color. The handle does not shade off into the bow as ours do but ends in a wide topped metal ferrule, which sometimes is still further broadened by a little projection, on which the arrow rests instead of on the hand. Quite often the bow is made in two parts that screw together in the handle. They use much more powerful weapons than we do. The weakest that I have seen were about 60 pounds in weight while many are fully 80 pounds and some are said to be as much as 100. An artistic feature, often introduced, is the carving of the top horn into the semblance of some animal, bird or reptile's head.

The arrows are very much thicker than ours and of different appearance. They are strongly chested and have a large horn head which may be an inch thick at its base. The shaft swells out to make a smooth joint with the thick pile so that the whole end has a sort of bulbous look. The shaft is never painted and the feathers are fastened on, not by glue, but by bright colored silk thread.

The archers that I have met had never heard of the "Point of Aim" as we understand the term, and seemed to scorn the idea. They shoot as the English did before the time of Ford, fixing the eye on the gold and drawing to the ear. The accompanying illustration is from a snap shot of a member of "La Compagnie de St. Sebastien" at Chantilly. It shows the draw to the ear, or at least in the line of that organ, and also shows the release by opening the fingers, as our Miss Wesson does, rather than by contracting them, as most of the rest of us do.

The shooting is sometimes at a popinjay, or at several of them placed on iron branches at

A BELGIAN ARCHER
Note the loose and point of draw

the top of a pole which may be, according to a Parisian paper of May 20th, 1913, which is in my possession, as much as 30 metres in height. One bird is higher than the rest and is called "Le Coq."

Usually a target is set up for the mark, as with us, but the freedom of our ranges is lacking. Instead of a spacious green lawn the general arrangement is more that of a shooting gallery for practice with firearms. There are two sheds, fifty metres apart and open on the sides toward each other. In one the archer stands and in the other is a butt against which the target face is fastened. All the shooting is at the one distance of 50 metres. Each man shoots one arrow and then gives place to his successor. A marker, who is protected by a screen, draws forth the shaft after each shot and calls back the result. At Chicago, where I saw the Belgian archers, most of the men had brought only one arrow to the range with them. Mr. Wallace Bryant, of Boston, who has shot with the archers of Paris and who is especially well qualified to judge, says that the skill they display is extraordinary, nearly all the arrows hitting the center.

According to the French paper quoted above, the name of which is torn off, the chief prize in the grand annual tournament is five thousand francs.

Early in the war some of the Belgian archers shot messages across the border into Holland and it was reported that one of these shafts hit a Dutchman in the neck.

Of course the very territory that Continental archery flourished in is the one where the war is raging most fiercely. Let us hope that the great conflict will not wipe the sport out forever in a locality where its hold has been so popular and strong.

CHAPTER XIX

Choice of Woods for Bowmaking

By James Duff

IT IS not our intention to mention in these pages any of the dozens of different kinds of wood that have been called into private use for bowmaking; but rather to confine the article to what may be termed standard woods in use by the craft, such as Yew, Lemonwood, Lancewood, Washaba and Osage-Orange; these all having been tried and found suitable for the purpose.

YEW

This wood has long been known as the best of all bow woods, for, given a straight grained stave of suitable length, free from pins and damp-sap, one has the makings of as nearly a perfect bow as it is possible to obtain. The pins can easily be seen as black spots in the wood and the damp-sap as a bluish line just under the white sap, or back, and running its whole length.

Wide, or coarse, grained yew is flabby and lifeless and unfit for bowmaking. It is also rather liable to chrysal, or even fracture, without any apparent reason.

Throughout almost the whole of the United States, usually on the hills and mountains, the wood grows in various quantities and qualities, but, unfortunately, it is generally of the shrub and bush variety and useless for the bowyer's purpose. It can be found in tree form on the western ranges of mountains, while in the East, on the Catskill hills, single yews can be seen growing in isolation; not in clumps as in the West. It is said by a well known woodsman, who has travelled the United States all over, that Georgia abounds in yew; and we know that in South America it is rather prolific, and that tons of it are shipped every year to the Swiss carvers, as can be seen in the well known cuckoo clocks. So it would seem that yew is not so scarce a domestic wood as one might imagine.

The Names "Spanish" and "Italian" can be taken in these days to be descriptive of any kind of yew that is of very fine growth, but not to indicate a product of Italy or Spain. It is very doubtful if one would be recompensed today for a tour of the once famous yew belt; for example the Apennines were virtually depleted many years ago, so that the *tasso nasso*, or yew, has become almost unknown there.

In selecting the wood, the bowyer will do well to avoid the female tree, if a choice be possible, as, in nearly every case, it will be of inferior grade when made into a bow. It takes nearly twice as much wood to make a bow of a given weight as does the male. A careful examination of the leaves of the tree will show at once if it be female, either by the presence of scarlet berries, or by the marks of where they have been when in seed; characteristics wholly lacking in the male tree.

Bowyers have been taught by experience that it is immaterial whether they cut down the tree in the fall or in the spring, as the result is the same in the finished bow.

The best trees are found on the hills and mountains, where the ground is dry, or where the water washes past the roots and does not lie soaking.

One should mark carefully, before cutting down, the side of the tree which is exposed to the north, as therein lies the best part.

Lemonwood and Lancewood

A common error among archers is that of confusing lemonwood with lancewood, for, as a matter of fact, they are entirely different. Let us consider the following statement by Mr. C. D. Mell, acting dendrologist to the Office of Forestry, Washington, D. C.

"Lemonwood, botanically known as *Psychetria eckloniana*, a species of *Rubiaceae*, is native to Cape Colony and often grows to the height of 30 feet, and from 2 to 3 feet in diameter. The wood is very hard, tough and useful. Lancewood (Black), so much used for carriage shafts, bows, etc., is botanically known as *Guatteria virgata Dun*. There is, however, a related wood, *Duguetia guitarensis*, native to Cuba and Guiana, which is also called lancewood, and although this is light (yellow) and very elastic, it is seldom used for bows, but is principally imported for the use of coach builders."

Lemonwood is the wood of which perhaps 75% of the bows in use are made. There are several reasons why this kind of bow should hold a high place, chief among them being the fact that several bows may be had for the cost of one of yew. Were it not that lemonwood has a tendency to follow the string, or take a set in the drawing direction, it would be considered as good as yew in every respect; but that set is inevitable, and, while it does not detract from the shooting quality of the bow, it certainly does not add to its appearance.

That one need never hesitate to adopt lemonwood bows for shooting because of any supposed inferiority to those of yew, is nowadays generally accepted. We know that nearly all previous records have been broken by archers using them and that some of the most noted archers today use nothing else; getting as good results and as much satisfaction as though indulging in the most expensive yew.

Lancewood, though somewhat similar in appearance to lemonwood, is of a different nature altogether and is much harder to work. As a guide to the buyer it is generally stained a rich, brown color with nitric acid. It has much more spring in it and is more likely to shiver into small pieces, even where the wood does not show a flaw. For target work it ranks low, as it jars the arm too much for accurate work, but it is certainly superior to yew and lemonwood for flight shooting.

Lancewood can be easily known by looking at the grain, which will be found to be shot, as in beechwood.

WASHABA

Washaba is a wood that is native to South Africa, and was but little known, outside of the bowmaking craft, until within recent years. It grows to a great height, often reaching 80 feet, and has been known to show a girth of 9 feet. Unfortunately there are two qualities of Washaba, one that is nearly perfect, straight grained and smooth, and one that is twisted in grain and very coarse. The difference between the two is caused entirely by the conditions of growth. The trees that are exposed to the great gales on the coast of Africa are all wind-twisted, that is, they are distorted in shape while growing and, as a result, become almost useless for bowmaking, the grain of the wood seldom running two inches alike. On the other hand the trees that are sheltered are all straight in grain and make almost ideal bows, especially where one seeks the sharp cast and long distance is desired.

Bows made of this wood are not to be compared to those made of the woods already mentioned, because they must be backed to be of any use, the best material for that purpose being straight grained second growth Hickory. They are rather more trying to the bow arm than either Yew or Lemonwood, and are, therefore, not recommended for the fine work of the shorter ranges. For the longer distances they are excellent weapons, inasmuch as the sharper cast allows of a flatter trajectory and, as a result, the shooter has the advantage of a much lower point of aim.

A Washaba bow of 54 pounds weight has been observed by the writer to carry an arrow 200 yards, flying almost flat, which, at the end of that distance, penetrated a steel shield $\frac{1}{16}$ inch thick for four inches, without breaking.

The value of this wood has been recognized within the last few years by the makers in the fishing tackle trade and today most of the best surf casting rods carry a top piece made from Washaba, or Bethabara as it is known to the rod maker. These top pieces are very slender and from six to ten feet in length and are required to carry very heavy game fish. They are also very costly.

Osage Orange

This wood is native to North America and can be found throughout the United States, although most of it is of the shrub variety. Where it is long enough for the purpose of bow making it is apt to be too crooked to be of much value. However, even though they are not plentiful, yet quite a few good trees may be had, and, as the Osage Orange is not known to be marketed, probably the wood may be had for little or nothing.

If given a piece of Osage Orange that is good enough for the purpose of making a bow, the maker will produce a fairly good weapon, inasmuch as the cast is superior to anything outside of Washaba. Besides, the bow will be found to always retain its shape and the recoil does not take so much out of the bow arm as does that of Washaba, although it is a little greater than in Lemonwood. For this reason it may be called into use as an all round bow for every distance. The weather does not affect this wood as it does the more famous kinds, therefore, when once his point of aim has been secured, the shooter need not fash about the heat or cold, as with yew. This wood may be backed with either Hickory or Elm, as it is very tough, but the self bow gives the most satisfaction, if it can be procured.

Bow Woods and the Weather

Of all the woods mentioned above, Yew is most affected by the weather. Sudden changes in the temperature, or in the barometric pressure, may cause well defined alterations in the cast. Yew is also more inclined to tire than other woods, yet, in spite of these drawbacks, the smooth feeling and easiness of draw, the almost unfelt recoil at the loose and the sharpness of cast all make the Yew the most valuable weapon.

Lemonwood tires a little less than Yew but heat and cold affect its cast almost as much.

Lancewood does not tire readily, has a better cast than either Yew or Lemonwood, and, with Osage Orange and Washaba, is not easily affected by the weather.

CHAPTER XX

Bows and How to Make Them

By J. M. Challiss

THERE comes a time in the life of every archer, if he is of a mechanical turn, when he is not satisfied with the commercial bow which is available at moderate cost, nor is his proficiency sufficient to justify the expenditure necessary to procure a really good weapon, when he naturally inquires "Why cannot I make a bow?" and finding no serious opposition to his inquiry he proceeds to explore a very interesting field. If he is self taught and has never had the benefit of contact with real archers, or if he has only seen or used the imitation bows that are sold at curio shops as genuine Indian bows, his attempts at bow making are pathetic. And yet there is hardly any form of bow that the mind can conceive, or an amateur turn out that will not find its counterpart in the collection of Joseph Jessop, of San Diego, Cal., who has collected bows from all climes and all peoples. It is strange to note the fundamental

Photo. by Pearce

Annual Tournament, N. A. A., Haverford, Pa., 1914

principles that will guide a savage race in the fashioning of their bows, or rather the fashions they will follow. Many of them are diametrically opposed to what has been selected as the last word in bow construction among civilized peoples, and what experience has shown to be the best form to be followed. Yet these people who rely upon the bow in many instances for their sustenance find that their odd and misshapen weapons shoot and shoot hard. To sum the whole matter up a bow is simply a piece of wood, horn or metal, bent by the aid of a string and which propells an arrow by its tendency to assume its original position. Any stick that will bend will cast an arrow, some better than others. If the stick is fashioned in a certain shape it will cast the arrow better than if it is unformed, and this form constitutes the science and art of bow making. Modern archers have settled upon a bow that is flat on the back, round on the belly, gradually tapering to the tips and of about six feet in length as the desideratum. This is commonly known as the long bow. The bows of many savage tribes are much longer and a larger percentage of them much shorter. The much overestimated American Indian archer used a shorter bow.

There is nothing intricate about bow making. Compared with the art of the fletcher it is like breaking sticks. You can make a bow out of most anything and in any form. Some are better than others, that is all. In the following remarks it is our purpose to give some simple directions, which if followed by one with slight skill and much care and patience, will result in turning out a conventional bow along English lines. The material out of which you will make your bow is the important question. If you consult the ordinary book or article on bows they will tell you that bows are made out of "yew, washaba or lance." That is very good. Where are you going to get the material? Did you ever see a tree of such? My Century Dictionary does not even tell me what washaba is. You can buy these expensive and imported woods in the large cities, but we do not all live in the large cities. That being the case we have to use what we have at hand, and when we look over our possessions we are surprised to find the wealth of material we have at hand. A good bow can be made of many of the native American woods, and the best in the world out of Oregon yew. I say best for the reason that it has been proven in actual contest that they will shoot as well as the imported English and Italian yew bows and last longer. But then we do not all live in the Oregon mountains where this wood is obtainable, so we must look some where else. We do not have to look far, for in fact any wood will make a bow. Of course some is much better than others, but the fact remains that with proper attention given to the grain of the wood and sufficient length provided a bow can be made out of the most brittle wood. But, of course, a bow of nine feet in length would be out of the question, and that would be the length you would have to make your bow in order to use some of the woods we have at hand. The most common wood that is used for boys and Indian bows is hickory, but there are other woods easily obtained that are much better. After use hickory seems to lose its cast, due to the fibre of the wood becoming crushed in the belly of the bow. You know that every time a bow is drawn to its capacity the fibre in the belly is crushed or pressed together while that in the back of the bow is pulled and stretched. Hickory will stand this pulling but fails when it comes to the crushing test. This characteristic of hickory is taken advantage of by bow makers when they make what is called a backed bow or one made of two pieces of different woods. They select for the belly a wood that will stand crushing, as for instance red cedar, the sweet smelling kind that is used for making pencils, and hickory for the back, and produce a bow that is as good as the best. But then we have not come to that yet. We will tell you about backed and grafted bows later on.

If you have access to growing timber you can select your own bow material, and thus, have the advantage of the city dweller who will have to get his at the lumber yard or wagon shop and be compelled to put up with old and brash wood which in all probability will be kiln dried and consequently ruined. Select a sapling or young tree of from three to five inches in diameter, the trunk of which is straight and free from knots or limbs. In making your selection you can take either mulberry, black locust, sassafras, apple, black walnut, osage orange, elm, ash, hemlock, dogwood, and if you find nothing better, hickory. Among these woods mulberry and black locust are considered the best, but you are not justified in refusing to use any kind of wood you can get that has a long straight grain and that is not notoriously brittle. Experiment, and you might find a better bow wood than has been heretofore discovered. When you have selected your sapling cut a piece from the trunk not less than six feet long. The length of your bow will depend upon your size and strength. Your bow should be as long as you are tall, but at least six feet long. For a youth fourteen or fifteen years of age the bow should be five feet and three inches or better still five feet and a half. A short bow is liable to break, and while it has a "snappy" cast, it is not pleasant to use. A safe rule is to make your bow of such length that you can easily brace, or string, it by the method to be hereafter explained. After securing your tree trunk you must remove the bark and then saw the piece lengthwise through the middle. This will give you material for two bows, and if you have selected a sapling large enough you can saw each half through the middle and will then have four quarters for the same purpose. You will find that there is a marked difference between the heart and sap of the wood, both in looks and quality and we will take advantage of this fact later on. Of course the wood we have is green and unseasoned and before we use it we will have to season it. This is done by finding a running stream of water, if we can, and by weighting our sticks we keep them in the water for from two to six weeks, depending upon their size and the nature of the wood. A wood with a close compact grain will require more time than one with an open porous grain. The theory in this method of seasoning, and it is proven in practice, is that the sap in the wood is supplanted by the water, and when the water is subsequently driven out the grain of the wood is left tough and elastic, rather than dry and brittle, as would be the case if the wood was allowed to season in the air. This is shown by the fact that kiln-dried timber is almost invariably brash and liable to fracture upon the slightest strain. Of course if you cannot find a stream to immerse your sticks in you will have to put them in a trough, tank or cistern. Running water simply accelerates the elimination of the sap. Of course if you live in the city and have to buy your bow material you will get it already seasoned, but be sure you do not get kiln-dried if you can possibly help it. Osage orange makes a good bow but it is very liable to weather check, and when seasoned is hard to work. Cedar is also good, but it is very hard to secure pieces of sufficient length, free from knots. I have made a most excellent bow from a piece of sassafras secured from a two inch board sixteen inches wide. A sapling of this wood should make a desirable bow.

While our material is seasoning we will discuss the size of our bow. The strength, and consequently the casting power of a bow is determined by the number of pounds it is necessary to pull upon the string in order to pull it back the full length of the arrow and called weight. This statement, as far as the casting power of a bow is concerned is only partially true as some bow woods are much quicker than others, and with two bows of equal weight, i. e., pull, but made of different woods one is liable to have a farther cast. It is this characteristic that makes yew so valuable, not this alone, however, as snakewood has a quicker cast, but is rejected by veteran archers on account of being heavy, and its liability to jar and fragility. A bow for a man should range in weight from 35 to 70 pounds, depending upon the individual and whether the bow is for target shooting or hunting. The main thing to be guarded against is to not get a bow that is too strong for the shooter. To shoot with a bow beyond your strength results in poor scores, sore fingers and ultimate disgust and condemnation of a pastime, the beauties of which you have denied yourself in attempting to impress upon your fellows that you were possessed of superior physical prowess. The best archers use a bow many pounds lighter than they are capable of using. Archery is not a test of strength, but of skill and the intelligent use of such powers as we possess. Of course as the archer masters his bow he will increase in strength and should in just that proportion increase the weight of his weapon.

The weight of a bow is determined by its length, the amount of material left in it and the quality of the wood. The hard dense woods such as ash, hickory and osage orange will require less bulk than the softer woods such as sassafras or cedar. In all probability your bow will range in size from ¾ inch to 1⅛ inch square at the largest part. A lance wood bow 1 inch square will weigh 65 pounds while a sassafras bow of the same size would weigh about 25 pounds. The shorter a bow of given size the more it will weigh. We cannot determine in advance just how large the finished bow will be but will have to ascertain that by experiment and repeated trials, so a safe rule is to make your bow larger than you have reason to believe will be acceptable and then reduce it to correspond to your strength.

After your stick has been taken from the water, wiped off and dried in the shade for three or four days and then hung up over the kitchen stove for a week it will be ready to work upon. For your first trial select your poorest stick to practice upon. If it is a success in the first instance you have in reserve a better stick more thoroughly seasoned from which you can make a better and stronger bow as you increase in skill and strength. After determining the length you want your bow, measure your stick and cut a piece as long as you want the bow to be from nock to nock, that is if you intend to use horn tips, but if it is your intention to cut notches in the bow itself to carry the string then you must cut your stick four inches longer than you want the finished bow. The sap of the wood is tough and elastic, it must be used for the back while the more dense heartwood is used for the belly. Square up the edges of your piece with a drawing knife so that it may be firmly held in the vise with the sap uppermost, in doing so you can shave it down until it is 1⅛ inches wide, but do all of this work on the edges, not on the sap or heart of the stick. Now comes the important part and the durability and life of your bow depends upon your careful attention to this feature of its manufacture. Now place your stick, which by this time has been reduced by the drawing knife and its two sides planed smooth with the jack-plane, in the vise with the sap uppermost. Study the grain of the wood. Does it run true, flat and even, or does it dip and thicken up in places, if it dips, does the same increased thickness show upon both sides of the stick? Now we must reduce this sap so that we will leave a layer from ⅛ to 3/16 of an inch in thickness along the back of our bow, and in doing so we must follow the grain of the wood as nearly as possible. Of course any slight wave or depression we can ignore, and make our back practically level and flat, but if we encounter a pronounced bend or depression in the grain of the wood we must follow it. In other words a bow which has the grain of the wood "running out" or cut across on the back will not last. The cheap lance and lemonwood bows are finished with the back perfectly smooth, while at a meeting of the National Archery Association will be found bows costing as high as one hundred dollars and made of yew in which the back is far from straight, owing to the grain of the wood being followed in their making. However the sides of these are, and all bows should be, perfectly straight, so that when they are strung up and you look along the string and at the belly of the bow the string divides the bow equally.

Now if you have followed the instructions above given you have a billet of wood $1\frac{1}{8}$ inches wide, with a layer of sap along its entire length of about $\frac{3}{16}$ inch in thickness and more or less rounding, depending upon the size of the sapling in the first instance. If this convexity is too pronounced the centre may be slightly reduced so as to make the back almost flat, that is, flat across the grain. Now measure your stick and find its centre and mark it. From this point make a mark 1 inch above and 3 inches below. This is for the handle. Mark these last two points by drawing lines squarely across the back of the stick, and, of course, four inches apart. With a chalk line pulled very taut mark the centre of the back from end to end. At both ends of the stick mark a point $\frac{5}{16}$ inches from either side of the chalk mark. Draw lines with a straight edge from these points to the ends of the cross lines which you have used to mark the handle. Now with the drawing-knife at first and plane afterwards reduce the sides of your stick to these marks, and have the sides at right angles to the plane of the back.

Now turn your stick on its side and mark a point at either end $\frac{5}{8}$ of an inch from the back, and 1 inch from the back at either end of the handle, connect these points with a line. Then reduce the heart of the stick in the same manner you reduced the sides. You now have a stick $\frac{5}{8}$ inch square on the ends and the centre of which is 1 x 1$\frac{1}{8}$.

The handle, so far untouched, should be rounded on the inside, care being taken from now on that the back remains untouched, and should be made as large as can be conveniently held in the hand, and noticeably larger than the largest part of the finished limbs of the bow. When the bow is fully drawn it should not bend, even the slightest, in the handle, for this reason we are compelled to leave a lot of wood at this point. The measurements we have been working to we will find are for a bow probably stronger than we can pull, but we have taken this precaution in order to get our handle large enough, and having secured that necessary condition we will proceed to reduce the size of each limb by planing them on the belly and sides down to the required size. These measurements will vary somewhat depending upon the kind of wood we are using. The corners of the belly are rounded and planed off so that a section of the bow at any point if sawed through would look like a letter U which was almost if not quite as deep as it was wide; for instance if one of the limbs was 1 inch wide and $\frac{7}{8}$ inch deep at the largest part it would be probably $\frac{1}{2}$ inch wide and

$\frac{7}{16}$ deep at the ends. It will be impossible to plane the belly to within 4 or 5 inches of the handle, as to do so would make it the same size of the limbs, when it should be at least a quarter of an inch deeper, so at this point it will be necessary to carefully taper the handle into each limb by the use of the drawing knife, spoke shave, rasp or scraper. The handle may be wider than the limbs, however, without harm.

In reducing the belly of the bow we must be careful to follow the lines of the bow as determined by the back. The back is the base line from which we work, and if there is a kink or depression in it we must have a corresponding bulge or raised place in the belly. Another thing to bear in mind is that if we encounter a knot of small proportions, commonly called a pin knot, we must not condemn the stick and throw it away, as we may save it by doing what is called "raising" the knot, that is, leave the knot and the surrounding wood higher than the limb on either side of the knot. Many excellent bows are thus constructed. They look rough at rest but in use bend with a graceful curve if properly made.

The ends of the bow will be finished by filing with a small rat-tail file notches on either side for the string, care being taken to leave no sharp corners that are liable to cut, or placing horn tips thereon, as fancy dictates. If you want horn tips, and they are the most satisfactory, secure two inches from the tip of a cow's horn and drill a one-eighth inch hole in the larger end and one inch deep. Make a reamer of flat steel one inch long running to a point and as wide at the base as the tips of your bow. Sharpen the edges of this reamer with a file at an angle similar to the blade of a pair of scissors and having left a shank, on your reamer put it in a brace and ream out the hole in the horn to fit the ends of your bow which will be sharpened like a pencil to fit the tips. Sharpen a hard wood stick to fit in the tips and clamp the stick in the vise and with rasp, file and scraper fashion the tip to suit your fancy. File a notch in the tip to hold the string, making it round and smooth and at such an angle that the string will rest on the bottom of the notch when the bow is strung. The top of the notch should be cut away so that when the bow is fully drawn it will not interfere with the string. If the horn works too hard it may be softened by boiling. Finish with emery paper.

The horn tips may be securely fastened on the ends of the bow with glue.

To brace or string the bow slip the eye of the string over the upper end and fasten the lower end with a timber hitch, so that the eye will be about two and one-half inches below the upper nock. The bow is strung by holding the lower limb with the inside of the foot, pulling upon the handle with one hand and depressing the upper limb with the other, at the same time slipping the eye of the string into the upper nock. Use either hand to grasp the bow at the handle as suits your convenience, and you will find that whichever hand you select you will use the foot on that side of the body to hold the lower limb.

Now examine the bow and see if it bends evenly throughout its entire length. Look along the back lengthwise and see if it bends even and flat or if it pulled out of shape by the string. If the latter is the case and the string does not cut the middle of the bow it will be necessary to cure this defect by scraping that side of the belly which is opposite the portion of the back which is bulged out; in other words, scrape the low side of the belly. Do this very gradually and carefully and closely watch the result of your efforts. If one limb bends more than the other the stronger limb must be reduced to correspond. Remember the handle must not bend in the least and each limb must bend with an even graceful curve from the handle to the tip. After getting the bow to bend to suit you it must be weighed. To do this adjust your string so that when the bow is braced it will stand from 6 to 6½ inches from the inside of the handle, and with a spring balance draw the string, at its centre so that it will be 27 inches from the inside of the handle. If the spring balance shows that the bow weighs the required amount, well and good, if it is stronger than you want then the bow must be lowered or weakened by scraping it evenly throughout its entire length, taking off but little at a time and frequently testing to see that we do not go too far, and being careful that we scrape one side as much as the other in order to preserve the balance. Another way to test the bow is to weigh out in a sack as much sand or soil as necessary to give you the desired weight, and tie it up and affix a hook thereon. Drive two very stout nails at a convenient height above the floor and 4 inches apart; mark a point on the wall 27 inches below these nails; hang your bow on these nails by the handle and hook the bag of sand in the centre of the string. When the bag of sand will pull the string down to the mark you have a bow of the required weight. Of course in making this test or the one with the spring balance you must not allow the bow to be under strain any length of time; hang on your weight, ease it down to the point where the bow will hold it, note the distance and immediately remove the weight.

To finish the bow it must be rubbed perfectly smooth with sand paper or steel wool, and the pores of the wood filled with a filler if necessary. Three coats of rubbing varnish or Chinamel, well rubbed between each coat should give a nice finish. If the handle is large enough, and of such shape as to feel pleasant to the hand nothing additional will be required beyond the trimming, however if it is small and hard to grasp it must be increased in size and improved in shape by glueing upon the back a piece of pine as long as the handle and nicely rounded. The trimming will be a piece of green or red plush glued around the handle, or any other material that suits your taste. In locating the handle you must remember that it is not in the exact centre of the bow but between the marks we put on the back as guides, which results in the upper limb being longer than the lower. This disparity in length causes the upper limb to bend more than the lower, so that if the bow when braced shows a very slightly increased bend in the upper limb it is not objectionable. Barnes, the famous American yew bowyer trims his handles with strips of split leather wound around the handle. A good covering would be a piece of calf skin, cut to fit, and sewed along the back with the base-ball stitch.

Soft wood bows should have a piece of ivory, mother of pearl or any other hard substance let into the left side of the upper limb just above the handle, to allow the arrows to glide over without wearing the bow at that point. This is called the arrow plate.

The bow which is now finished and ready for use is what is called a self bow, that is one made without a back. There is another kind of bow which is a self bow but is made of two pieces joined in the handle, and it is known as a grafted bow. As it is hard to get a piece of yew of sufficient length, and sufficiently clear of knots and pins to make a perfect bow, the grafted variety is very common in bows of that wood, and they are entirely satisfactory, that is if well made. Expert bowyers claim that there is a difference in the quality of the wood in either end of a six foot stick, and for that reason indorse the grafted bow for the reason that wood of the same quality and from a half length of the same stick may be placed in either limb of the bow, with uniform results. If you are unable to get a clear stick of sufficient length to make a bow you should have no difficulty in getting a stick of half that length, and large enough to get two limbs from it. Prepare your sticks by reducing the sap as you did for the bow just described, and select the butt end of the stick for the joint. To make the joint you must make the ends of your limbs perfectly square for a distance of four inches. This may result in cutting across the grain in the handle, but as the bow will not bend there and will be protected by a whipping it will be of no consequence. In squaring the ends you must remember that in the finished handle there must be left sufficient wood to give it rigidity. On the back of one of the limbs mark it in the shape of a W which is upside-down, as wide as the stick and at least three and one-half inches long; carefully mark the belly to correspond. Clamp the stick securely in the vise and with a fine saw cut out the V shaped piece in the middle and with drawing-knife and plane cut off the long triangular pieces on either side down to the outside mark. If you do not get this sawed out accurately it will be necessary to dress it up with a knife-edge file, using the utmost care to keep the surfaces flat and true. Saw two deep notches in the other limb, first marking them out, so that when finished the one limb will fit into the other and the sides of the two limbs be parallel. The two things to be watched in making this joint are to see that it is a perfect fit on both the back and belly, and that when the stick is joined it will be straight. This joint is called a double fish joint and is very strong. Now with the best glue that you can procure, the same having been put to soak in cold water over night, and then boiled in a glue pot, or water bath, and used while boiling hot, thoroughly coat the proposed joint getting the glue into every portion of the joint and fit the pieces together, driving them smartly home with a mallet, and clamp the joint very firmly in the vise until dry. In a day or two the glue will be sufficiently hard to allow you to work on the stick and reduce it to about the proper size and shape for the proposed bow. Now you will have to put a whipping of very stout cord or tape around the joint, starting well outside of the ends of the joint, winding close, smooth and as tight as your whipping will allow. This whipping should be laid on in glue, and after completed if it will not make too much bulk in the handle you should put on a double or triple whipping. There is a very severe strain on this joint and you cannot make it with too much care nor too strong. The more whipping you put on and the tighter you draw it the better will be your joint. Let the glue in this whipping dry at least a week before you attempt to brace the bow, which, of course, you have not attempted before the whipping was on. This bow will be finished the same as the former one excepting that the whipping will receive repeated coats of varnish to make it absolutely water-proof.

The backed bow is a most excellent weapon and one in which hickory demonstrates its peculiar merit, as most all backed bows are made with such backs. To make one secure a piece of well seasoned second growth white hickory of the width and length you want your bow and when planed and smoothed up of three-sixteenth inch in thickness. Excellent backs may be secured by procuring from a carriage maker or hardwood dealer a buggy reach or coupling. These are six feet long and $1\frac{1}{4}$ inch square. By looking over a large stock you can most likely find several in which the grain is straight and even and does not run out, which when taken to the planing mill and ripped on a circular saw will afford material for three or four backs; use sharp saw. Carefully dress the back you select with a sharp fore-plane. The belly will be made substantially as wide as the back, at least in the centre, and of sufficient depth to leave plenty of wood in the handle. The back of the belly must be planed smooth, true and straight, and upon this planed surface the back must be glued. The surfaces to be glued should be combed with a fine toothed saw. The glueing process is the difficult part of the job. The glue must be of the best, in perfect solution and boiling hot. As soon as it is applied to every portion of both surfaces, immense pressure must be exerted upon the two sticks to force out all surplus glue. You can exert this pressure by means of wedges or cabinet makers clamps. If you use the former method nail two inch planks parallel to each other and about three inches apart on your bench and provide a series of short double wedges for the entire length of the bow and so arranged that the small square end of one is snug against the large end of the next one and so on. By driving the end wedge all are thus moved and a uniform pressure is exerted from end to end. If you use clamps use as many as you can put on, and clamp the bow, back down, to a two inch board. This board keeps the back straight while being glued on. Do not take the bow out of the clamps for a week. Dress down and finish as for a self bow.

It requires nice adjustment to make your wedges so that by driving the end wedge all will be equally tightened and you can get almost as good results by leaving a space of three-quarters of an inch between each set, and driving each wedge individually. They may be driven by a notched hard wood stick. Drive them all they will stand. To make a good glue joint immense pressure is necessary and you must remember this is making a grafted as well as a backed bow. In making the joint in the grafted bow if the jaws of your vise are not exactly as wide as the joint you should cut hard wood blocks just the length of the joint and place them on either side of the joint and clamp the whole in the vise. If the blocks are longer than the joint the solid wood will take the pressure that is intended for the joint. Another thing, while the back and belly are to be planed perfectly true and flat where they are to be glued, they should not be left smooth but the surfaces should be scored by scratching them lengthwise with a fine toothed saw, as explained. There are special planes made for this purpose. The roughened surface gives the glue a better opportunity to take hold.

While hickory, next to yew, is the best for backs there are several woods that are excellent for bellys. Among them are red cedar, the heart wood of black locust, black walnut, mulberry, osage orange, and sassafras.

While the directions herein given are general in their nature they are intended to cover the making of an ordinary sized bow for a man. Of course if the bow is wanted for a woman or a youth the length and size of the bow must be reduced accordingly, as well as the draw. The ordinary length of men's arrows are 28 inches and they require a bow of at least 6 feet in length. Among my bows I have one 3 inches over 6 feet, which weighs 65 pounds and it has stood a lot of hard usage in the wild. While we have given the weight of bows for men as ranging from 35 to 70 pounds the limits are not hard and fixed. For target use 45 pounds will be found to suit the average man. Many expert archers including Thompson, Taylor, Richardson, et al., use a heavier bow, at the targets, while other experts use lighter than the weight indicated. When hunting we require a much heavier bow, for the reason that the arrows are very much heavier than the fragile target arrow. They are weighed in ounces not shillings. Then the bow is more constantly used than at the targets, and there is no dwelling on the aim. The result is that we can without effort fully draw a bow that weighs 20 to 25 pounds more than the bow we are accustomed to use at the targets. If you have a good, well finished target bow do not run the risk of ruining it in hunting. You will scratch and mar it in the underbrush and the quick snappy draw you give when your game is sighted may result in its fracture. Make yourself a hunting bow of hard wood and follow the call of the wild. There is nothing like it.

CHAPTER XXI

Yew Bow Making

By Dr. Harold G. Goldberg

AMONG poets the yew tree has become synonymous with the weapon which is made from it and thus we read of the twanging yew, the yew obedient to the shooter's will. "Sons of Luth," says Ossian, "bring the bows of our fathers, let our three warriors bend the yew." So it is not only true that the yew has always been associated in history with the long bow, but down to the present time no other wood has ever been found in bow-making to take the place of this classic tree. The tree, *taxus baccata*, is an evergreen which sometimes attains great size. According to the encyclopaediac descriptions, "specimens of remarkable antiquity are commonly seen in old church yards. The timber is extremely durable and valuable and was formerly much used in making bows. Its leaves and young branches act as an acrid poison when eaten by man and the lower animals. It seems to be a native of almost every country of a temperate climate, the finest specimens being found in Spain and Italy." Wood from these two countries was so well known and held in such high regard in England that during the reign of Edward IV a law was devised compelling the wine merchants of Spain and Italy to deliver a certain number of yew staves with every cask of wine imported into England. In the United States the yew is found in the State of Oregon and in many other parts. Some of the finest specimens of the wood have been taken from the Cascade mountains of Oregon. The tree is cut during the months of November, December, January and February when the sap is down and then split and seasoned in the log. It is in this form that it is generally supplied by the dealers.

Yew bows are of two principal kinds, self and backed. The former is made up of two single sections of wood, joined at the handle, while the latter is made up of two sections of wood joined at the handle, each section composed of two or more pieces of wood or other substances glued together longitudinally. Yew bows are made of two sections of wood rather than of one continuous piece because it is desirable to secure two limbs of as nearly the same growth as possible. Were the stave of one piece, one limb would be of different density than the other, owing to the difference in the age and development of the two parts. The belly of the bow is always the rounded portion nearest the shooter, during the act of drawing and the back is the opposite surface, a flat arc, always white in color. The color of the belly of a yew bow varies from a deep chocolate shade to a golden yellow, the color commonly seen being a light yellowish red.

Of all the woods used in the manufacture of the self bow, yew is the wood *par excellence*. It is light in the hand, sweet of cast, steady of aim and has great propulsive power. To obtain a perfect piece is such a difficult matter that one is scarcely ever seen. A perfect stave should possess a fine, close grain which should be even and straight, the line of demarcation between the white sap and red heart should be well defined, and not thickened by a blur of purplish discoloration which in some cases is evidence of decay. It should be free from knots, pins, curls, season checks, galls, wind checks and pitch pockets. Do not let the amateur bow-maker be discouraged, however, by this detail of imperfections, because very good bows may be made from staves exhibiting many of these faults. It is just such difficulties in fact, that the bow maker must encounter, that makes the art of bow making so fascinating, while the planning of a bow from an imperfect stave incites the ingenuity and skill of the maker to a point of greater endeavor. Were a piece of wood without the imperfections enumerated easily obtainable, anyone without even an ordinary amount of skill and with few tools might turn out a very serviceable bow. Such not being the case, however, the various faults must be met with each in its turn and conquered in a way best adapted to each individual piece. The tools needed in bow making are as follows: A hatchet, cross-cut saw, rip saw, jack plane, finishing plane, large and small spokeshave, a Stanley scraper, a coarse and fine file, a glue pot suspended in a water bath, and a vise workbench.

The log-sections are generally 3 feet 6 inches long by 6 or 8 inches wide by 3 or 4 inches in thickness. The bark is first removed and if the log is fairly straight in grain and has not many bumps or knots upon its outside or sap surface, it is cleft its entire length with a hatchet. Should the grain appear to twist or turn, which may be determined by comparing its two extremities, it is safer to saw it in as nearly a straight line as possible. Before either of these operations is attempted, the line of cleavage should first be determined with due regard for the irregularities upon its sap surface, so that the limb should be as flat and straight upon its back as possible and finish at the extremities with the lines of separation between the sap and heart parallel to each other. It will require, as a rule, careful observation to obtain this result, but the effort is well repaid as the subsequent steps of the process are much simplified.

Perhaps of all the woods from which bows are made the yew is the most uncertain in quality. A beautiful log may turn out the most disappointing staves, so the beginner must not be discouraged by such results, if he ever expects to succeed, as these logs are almost certain to be met with; most likely upon the first occasion.

The limb now having been produced, we proceed to shape it. The sides are first straightened with a jack plane until the block is 1½ inches in thickness. It is then set in the vise and the back formed. This is a very important step in bow making and great care must be exercised to obtain the necessary result. Taking the actual plane of the tree, which in the log is of course slightly rounded, as the plane of the back to be established, the spokeshave is drawn carefully backward and forward until the sap has been reduced throughout its entire length to ¼ inch in thickness. This will produce a barely perceptible curve which is to be retained until the finish of the bow. The curve of the limb must be followed, the tool dipping with the depressions in the heart, preserving the same proportion of sap to heart the whole length, i. e., ¼ inch in thickness.

Often it will be found that the sap dips more deeply into the heart upon one side of the limb than the other. In this case the side upon which the sap is thinnest must be selected and the peculiarities of the wood followed upon this side. In such a case should the sap upon the opposite side dip very deeply into the heart, the ¼ inch may be sacrificed somewhat for the sake of flattening the general plane of the back, otherwise our relation of sap to heart would be considerably out of proportion. Except in the white portion, yew is a very soft wood, in spite of what some text books would lead us to believe. It is compact, but of about the cutting consistency of white pine. We must therefore use great caution with our spokeshave, working carefully in both directions, following the leaves or feathers of the grain, as they run first in one direction and then in the other. A too vigorous stroke will sometimes raise a sliver of wood that will penetrate so deeply that our stave may be ruined.

Having shaped the two limbs about $1\frac{1}{2}$ inches in thickness and established our back a flat arc $\frac{1}{4}$ inch in thickness, at a perfect right angle to our roughly planed sides, we now proceed to cut the splice. This is accomplished as follows: A piece of drawing paper is obtained, being somewhat thicker than ordinary writing paper and two parallel lines are drawn upon it. Our splice is to be a fish tail $3\frac{1}{2}$ inches in length by $1\frac{1}{4}$ inches in width. This is marked out upon the paper.

The lines are divided with a knife and separated, and the two sections thus formed pasted one upon each limb at its extremity. We have first decided which extremity this is to be, selecting the end of the limb containing the greater number of imperfections in the wood, since this portion of the finished bow is to be the thicker, and consequently less apt to fracture. The paper having been pasted upon the wood, sighting along the back to determine whether it is parallel to the sides, the limb is placed upright in a vise and we proceed to cut the splice. This step requires considerable skill as much depends upon its successful result. Taking the sharp rip saw we cut through the lines in the paper pattern, being careful to saw always in the same plane from top to bottom.

The splice cut, it must next be glued. For this purpose ordinary joiner's glue is selected, not cold prepared liquid glue. The glue is melted in the water bath until it is of the consistency of sugar syrup. If it is too thick the vise will squeeze the segments apart, while if it is too thin, the wood will absorb too much of it, so it is important to have it just right. It is better to set back, or reflex, the limbs somewhat from a straight line, about ½ inch being a safe angle, so before the glue is applied, the two limbs are fitted together and this angle marked with lead pencil as a straight line along both sides, well beyond each extremity of the splice. When the limbs are glued and joined after this we simply preserve the continuation of these straight lines and our splice is then at an exact angle we have determined that it should be. The splice is now covered upon all its surfaces with two or three coats of glue and placed in the vise, the sides of the limb protected, if the vise is of metal, by interposing a piece of soft wood between the jaws and the wood. It is squeezed tightly, not enough to crush the wood and allowed to remain for two days.

We now have a stave something more than 6 feet in length and it is time to proportion our bow. The stave is placed in the vise for the sake of convenience, the irregularity over the surface of the splice caused by setting back the limbs is shaved away, and the measurements are proceeded with as follows. Taking the 3½ inch splice as our basis of measurement, it is divided into half, marking a line in lead pencil, 1¾ inches from each of its extremities. The middle of the bow is to be one inch above the center of the splice, which point is also marked off in lead pencil. The rest of the operation is very simple. Lay a rule upon the back of the stave and measure off 3 feet from the line which has been placed 1 inch above the middle of the splice, i. e., that which is to be the middle of the bow, a mark is made upon each extremity of the stave, and the excess wood cut off. If a measurement is then made from each end of the splice to each end of the stave, it will be found that one limb is 2 inches longer than its fellow, which are proper proportions for a 6 foot bow.

(See diagram.)

The outline of the back of a yew bow differs from those of the denser woods, such as lemon and lance, in that instead of inclining in a sharp straight line from the handle to the extremity, the back is made broader, inclining very gradually from the handle until within about one foot of the extremity it inclines more rapidly, ending in a sharp point for the reception of the horn. It is very important to obtain this correct outline because were we to adopt the pattern of the denser wood bows, our yew would be entirely too whippy at the ends, requiring too much wood in the belly and favoring the formation of chrysals, which in time would surely end in the destruction of the weapon. It is in fact its peculiar shape combined with the different character of the wood which makes the yew so soft of cast and consequently easy on the shooter.

We now plane down the sides of our stave, much care being exercised at this time to avoid raising splinters, until it is perfectly straight and is from $1\frac{1}{8}$ to $1\frac{1}{4}$ inch in thickness, depending upon what the power of our bow is to be. About $1\frac{1}{8}$ is assumed to be a good general average for a bow varying in weight from 40 to 45 pounds. A pattern is now made of paste board, first outlined in lead pencil and then cut with a sharp knife of the exact proportions of what our back is to be. This is laid flat upon the back and with a pencil a line is drawn upon each side of the pattern marking the outline upon the wood which is to be followed with the plane. The next step is to form the belly of the bow. Taking the *middle* and *not* the ends of the handle, as is the usual custom, we measure off for a bow which is $1\frac{1}{8}$ inches in thickness at the handle $1\frac{3}{16}$ inches from the surface of the sap into the heart of the wood. We measure off $\frac{5}{8}$ inch from the sap surface into the heart at each extremity, and then draw an irregular line, assuming that the stave is irregular in form from one point to the other. If much wood remains beyond this line, for the sake of saving ourselves considerable labor it may be sawed off with the rip saw, keeping beyond the line somewhat to avoid error. From now on the spokeshave comes into use, first rounding the sides, gradually approaching the summit of the belly until a perfectly rounded form is obtained. This is the most difficult step in the whole process of the undertaking, as the grain of the wood varies so constantly that we must always be on the alert to follow its peculiarities. We may now take our Stanley scraper, it being no longer safe to continue the use of the spokeshave, and complete the form of the belly. Every curve in the back of the bow must be carefully followed. In shaping the belly, gradually tapering toward the end, pins must be raised; by this is meant leaving a little more wood over the surface of the small black points that appear in the wood. Any other imperfections must be provided for in the same way. As has already been stated, in choosing which end of the limb is to form the handle, we have paid due regard to the imperfections of the wood. Keeping in mind that the principal bend in the bow is between a point 17 inches from the handle to within 8 or 9 inches of the end, we adjust the limbs accordingly. To secure the splice a strip of soft wood somewhat wider than the back of the bow and 3½ inches in length is glued over the joint, pressed in the vise, allowed two days to dry, and finally rounded in shape with the plane and file until it takes the general symmetry of the

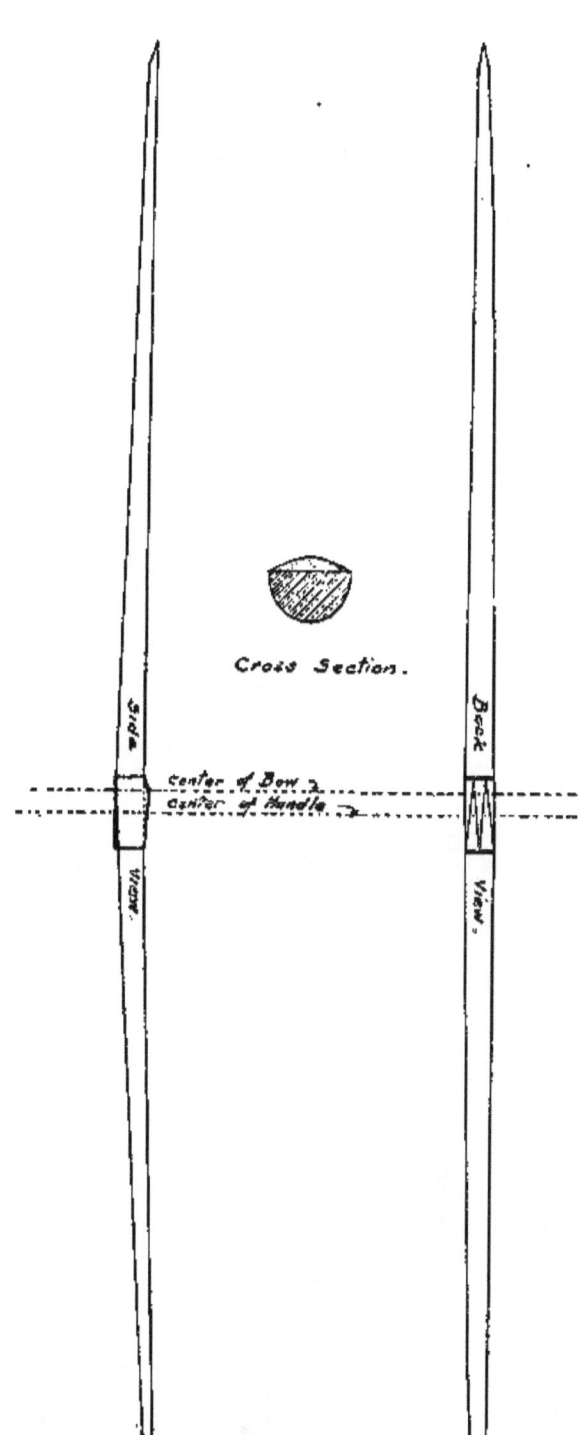

handle. It should have the same lines as upon the belly side, more wood being allowed to remain at the corresponding center than at either extremity, which end in a gradually sloping angle. (See illustration.) This must be further secured by wrapping it with a thin layer of raw flax saturated with joiner's glue and smoothed to an even surface. After this is dried hard and further shaped with a file, a coat of shellac is applied to render the joint moisture- and sweat-proof.

This method of centering the bow was suggested by Dr. S. T. Pope, of San Francisco, Cal., an expert amateur bow maker, and so far as the writer knows, the method originated with him. It seems the most effective scheme yet devised by any bow maker and having once handled a bow of such proportions, it will be found that it balances perfectly upon that portion of the hand into which it most comfortably rests, giving a steadier aim and allowing less chance for error in every detail.

The horns are next put on. Their openings should be $\frac{1}{2}$ inch in diameter, or not less than $\frac{7}{16}$ inch. They are carefully fitted to the end, filing away the wood until this is accomplished; cold (liquid) glue may be used to secure them in place. After they have dried, the bow is ready for tillering. The tiller is a staff of wood about 3 feet in length with a depression cut at its top to receive the middle of the bow, and notches cut down its face at intervals of several inches to a final depth of 26 inches. The tiller is placed upright in a vise and the bow braced. Before proceeding any further we turn the braced bow back up and then down, sighting first along one surface and then the other. This is to determine whether the back is perfectly flat and the string cuts the bow exactly into halves from notch to notch. Should the bow be cast to one or the other side, we may be assured that it is ill proportioned and that there remains too much wood upon the side toward which the deflection is formed. This is removed by means of the file or scraper. Now holding the bow at a transverse angle and satisfying ourselves that the curve of the limbs is about equal, the handle is placed upon the tiller and the string drawn to the first notch; in effect a great cross bow. As each successive notch is reached, gradually approaching the full draw, we step away from the tiller and observe the curve of the partially drawn bow. This observation must be made quickly, removing the bow each time, stringing and filing and scraping until a perfect arc is produced, and the exact weight which the bow is to remain has been decided. We now finish the bow with sand paper, steel wool and powdered pumice until all file marks have been removed and the bow has reached a fine smooth surface. After this it is rubbed to a polish with boiled linseed oil and the final dressing applied. This may be either shellac after the method of French polish or colorless varnish may be used in order not to darken the beautiful shades of the wood. The French polish is applied as follows: Dissolve white shellac in 95% grain alcohol, making a solution the consistency of syrup. Prepare a pad of cotton enclosed within a bit of gauze or cheese cloth. Dip it first in a dish of shellac and then in a dish of linseed oil; rub the surface of the wood vigorously. Repeat until a high, smooth gloss is produced. By this method only one coat may be applied and subsequent attempts to add to this will only mar the original coat. The first coat is rendered durable and sufficient by repeatedly rubbing the bow, several times during the season, with beeswax held in turpentine, or ordinary floor wax. If varnish be used, as many coats as desired may be applied and with the taste of the worker and placed upon the spot where the arrow crosses, excavating the wood just enough to receive it when it is glued into position.

Backed Bows

In describing backed bows, only two kinds will be considered, yew-backed-yew and rawhide-backed-yew. Backed bows were originally designed to make use of selected portions of wood which were considered unfit for self bows. Perhaps a heart was serviceable and the sap useless and vice versa. Bow makers then would put aside these staves until such times as they had obtained two perfect sections each of heart and sap and from these would make up their backed bows. In selecting wood fit for the backed bow, we must first of all have a perfectly even grained section of sap. It may be slightly curved in either direction but it must be straight of grain and at least ¼ inch in thickness with the side which is to be glued upon the heart perfectly smooth upon its surface. It must also be entirely free from knots, pins and other defects. This is carefully sawed from its defective heart with a rip saw.

In the case of the heart, however, we are allowed more scope in our selection. The grain need not necessarily be perfectly straight, since it is to be covered upon its back by the perfect reinforcement of sap and so we may utilize almost any kind of heart providing it is free from the glaring defects already described. It seems hardly worth while, however, to make a yew backed yew unless we have a heart free of all defects with the exception of an irregular grain, which may be entirely disregarded because it is generally possible to obtain such a piece free of blemishes, possibly a strip which has been sawed from one or more of our self bows, and which has been preserved for just this purpose. The heart section should finish in the block $1\frac{1}{2}$ inches in width by $1\frac{1}{8}$ inches in thickness, perfectly flat upon all its surfaces and preferably perfectly straight in form. We next make the two surfaces of sap and heart which are to be glued together exactly even, and this is not an easy matter but requires great care with the plane and file. The writer's method is to cut two blocks of some soft wood about 2 inches wide by 1 inch in thickness and as long as each limb. Now make transverse saw outs about 1 inch apart to a depth of $7/8$ inches, using these blocks for the press which is to be placed upon the limb after the sections have been glued. All our parts are now arranged in order upon the work table and the heart section is laid belly side down at the edge of the table and quickly covered with a coat of glue previously melted in the water bath. The sap is likewise glued, placed upon the heart and next the 2 inch block of soft wood upon the sap. The more tightly the two sections of sap and heart are squeezed together, the more firmly will they adhere and to effect this result without all the tools the professional bow maker has at his command, the writer has found that the small iron screw clamps which may be purchased at any five and ten cent store will serve very well. Enough of these are secured so that they may be placed about three inches apart, using the under surface of the table and the block of soft wood as the two surfaces against which the clamps are screwed. These are placed quickly, screwed into position with the fingers, and finally tightened with pliers. At the end of three days they may be removed and at the end of a few more days we may proceed with the further steps. These are the same as described in the case of the self bow.

Raw Hide Backed Yew

The writer will attempt to describe the method of Dr. S. T. Pope, of San Francisco, Cal., with apologies to Dr. Pope for any errors that may appear in the text. Dr. Pope maintaining that the sap wood serves no part in the cast of the bow entirely disregards any irregularities which may appear upon its surfaces in the formation of his back and planes the surface to a common level, in some cases entirely removing the sap if it is necessary to produce this result. In every other respect the bow is built in the usual way. The bow having been shaped and the proportions obtained within a few steps of the finished bow, the points are filed at the extremities to receive the horns, a little more wood being removed from the back of the point to allow for the strip of rawhide, and the stave is ready for its rawhide back. This is obtained from the tanners. It is a calf skin used principally by makers of artificial limbs and is about $\frac{1}{16}$ inch in thickness.

The hide is cut lengthwise into strips of 1½ inches in width. These are soaked in warm water for about ½ hour and are quickly painted upon their inner surfaces with melted glue. The limbs are treated in the same manner, the strips, first one and then the other are bound on at the handle, quickly stretched and bound at the tips. They are then smoothed and carefully bandaged their entire length with a gauze bandage. This dries over night and the overlapping edges are cut off with a pen knife and finished with a file. The horn tips are again fitted, glued, the handle piece of soft wood applied, bound, finished and shellacked and the bow is ready for tillering. This having been accomplished, it is sand papered, rubbed with steel wool and pumice powder, the rawhide sized with a thin layer of LePage's glue, rubbed with linseed oil and the bow finished in the manner previously described. While the writer cannot agree with Dr. Pope's contention that the sap plays no further part in the formation of the bow than a protection for the heart against fracture, he can enthusiastically commend the method to the bow maker, be he professional or amateur as one worthy of his best efforts. It is a far wiser and safer method for the beginner than either the self or yew backed yew and as for its shooting qualities, the writer has nothing more to say than that a beautiful fine grained dark mahogany yew bow made for him by Dr. Pope has stood the test of a season's shooting in the most delightful manner, finishing with no more loss of cast than one should expect to find in the finest bow, of any quality and without following the string to any excessive degree.

It is always best to allow the bow to remain idle for a year before it is put into active use for the sake of seasoning it in the form in which it is finished. The English bow makers take about five years in the manufacture of a bow, allowing one year to elapse between each step. While the writer cannot see any good reason for permitting so much time to these various steps, assuming that we are working on a stave already seasoned in the log, the fact remains that a well seasoned stave will give better results in the finished bow than a younger piece of timber. The wood darkens with age and in the bow increases in cast, so certainly some time should elapse between the finishing of the bow and the time it is put into use. Yew bows will follow the string to a certain degree and lose about 3 pounds in weight, no more, if the wood is properly seasoned and well proportioned. If the limbs are unequal in strength, the bow will lose cast and follow the string from this unequal strain, and will finally break; so all these points must be borne well in mind.

In conclusion let the writer say that he does not pretend to be a bow maker of any particular merit or even long experience. He does not claim that the methods mentioned are the best, but they are practical, and an attempt has been made to present them to the reader in a concise and comprehensible form, leaving nothing to be assumed. If he has succeeded in this, he will feel amply repaid for the effort. In this form they are offered to the reader with the hope that he will derive as much pleasure from their practice as the author.

"Thus when our sports are over,
In Autumn's final day,
Each Bowman sure will say;
Come, a parting cup,
Ay and bumper it up
To the next merry twang of the tough yew bow." (Dodd, 1818)

CHAPTER XXII

How to Make a Bow-String

By L. W. Maxson,

Seven Times Champion Archer of the United States

(Although the following article was printed in the *Archer's Register* for 1903, Mr. Maxson, shortly before his death, kindly furnished a manuscript copy for this book.)

TAKE best flax thread (Barbour's No. 12 preferred), and form three strands of fifteen threads each. Wax these and cut out the threads at one end to form an even taper eight or ten inches long. Form double tapers of a little more than twice this length and wax these to the main strands so as to lengthen the loops when completed. Lay the strands together and, beginning where the loop is to be formed, roll or twist each of the strands away from the body and lay the outermost over the others, drawing it firmly towards you. Continue this operation, always using the outer strand, till you have formed a cord long enough for the loop. Turn this back upon itself and wax down the tapered ends, each with one of the main strands of the string, arranging them so that they embrace one of the other strains. With the ends of the loop in close contact, resume the laying operation, "twisting from and drawing towards," till the cord has been laid beyond the filling pieces. Comb out the strands with the fingers, draw tight, and cut off about eight inches longer than the desired length of the bow-string, taper the ends and add strengthening sections as before.

At this point I generally catch the finished loop over the nock of the bow and drawing, the strands tight, begin to form the second loop about two inches short of the opposite nock. The second loop is formed exactly like the first, the three strands of the string being combed out as necessary, to prevent tangling. When the loops have been completed, wax together all the strands, partly twist them, and stretch upon the bow. Rub down with a piece of paper and repeat the twisting and rubbing till the portion of the string between the said sections becomes round and hard, and the bow is strung to the right height. A coat of varnish and proper serving complete as good a string as any archer needs. If the archer prefers, a silken serving may be laid on from loop to loop. For a ladies' bow three strands of thirteen threads are used.

A bow-string made as above seldom gives down, when once stretched, and may be adjusted in a moment by giving it a slight twist.

CHAPTER XXIII

NOTES ON ARROW MAKING

By Z. E. Jackson

THE construction of a good arrow requires attention to so much minutia and detail that it seems almost a hopeless task to attempt to describe the many operations in a single chapter. It will be understood in the beginning that this is not intended as a lexicon or an archery dictionary and if the weight of a bow is mentioned as being 50 pounds it does not mean that that bow, if laid upon the scales, would register 50 pounds in weight. Likewise, if an arrow is referred to as 4-6, meaning 4 shillings 6 pence, it does not refer to the cost of the arrow but to its weight. Where the superlative "best" appears it does not mean that the particular method or material referred to as being best is the best that the art or market has ever afforded, but is the best within the experience of the writer. If the name of a dealer in materials is used it is for the purpose of giving to the lovers of archery the benefit of much research in the market, and not for the purpose of advertising any particular firm.

One of the difficulties met by amateurs in the manufacture of their archery tackle is the lack of information as to where materials may be secured. If reference be made to some particular method adopted by commercial arrow makers it is for the purpose of comparison and not with the spirit of finding fault. I shall probably overlook many important details but no suggestion here made can be profitably omitted.

Of the numerous books on archery that I have read,—and my reading has covered practically the entire field—I have yet to find a single one that gave definite instructions that would be of benefit to the amateur. They all call attention to most of the requirements and then fail to state how to secure the necessary result. They speak of cutting a feather as though no more skill were required than in clearing the back yard of weeds. Glue is just glue without information as to which kinds are best adapted. English deal is referred to as a particular kind of wood, but so far as I am able to learn from inquiry of the tradesmen, deal is an English expression denoting dimension lumber. I might fill a chapter with reference to the generalities used by writers in attempting to describe the making of an arrow but it would be to no good purpose. I shall endeavor to set down what information I have secured in a long-continued effort to learn the mysteries and secrets of the old arrow makers and which they have apparently guarded with jealous care. I do not wish to be understood as saying that the methods described are the only methods which will give good results; what I do assert is that if the instructions are followed the product will be an arrow of which no man need be ashamed in field or tournament.

Inasmuch as there are many points of similarity between a target arrow and hunting arrow I shall first describe the method of making a target arrow and will then refer to such changes as are made necessary by the difference in use of the target and hunting arrow. I make no reference to the weights of either kind as that depends upon the individual choice and strength of the bow used.

The material used for the shaft of the target arrow is invariably some species of pine with a hard material for a nock to prevent splitting, and a wood harder and heavier than pine for the footing. In a fourteen years' search I have never been able to secure a good piece of pine. I have tried hard pine, yellow pine, Western pine, Southern pine, spruce and Oregon fir. A clear piece of close, vertical grain hard pine flooring is fair material, but the best American wood is Oregon fir, care being taken to select staves in which the grain is very fine and does not run out of a $\frac{3}{8}$ of an inch square stave in 28 inches. Needless to say, the material should be well seasoned but not kiln dried. Kiln dried lumber is as useless for archery tackle as driftwood. That end of the pine stave which will be footed is then planed down on two sides, a distance of $5\frac{1}{2}$ inches from the forward end and brought to a feathered edge of a thickness equal to the saw slot in the footing hereafter mentioned. This work is best done by hand and instead of placing the stave on a bench and planing it, the plane is held in an inverted position in the vise and the stave planed by drawing it over the plane. The pressure required bends the thin edge of the stave producing a result very much as in the hollow ground razor; that is, the edges of the wedge are not a straight line but a curve.

The footing may be of any hard, heavy wood. Beefwood does not work well under the plane; the grain is gnarly like maple. Snakewood makes a beautiful footing but does not hold the glue without special treatment. Lancewood does not give the desired contrast in color; mahogany is too light in weight; ebony is too brash; the many different kinds of rosewood are too light; amaranth is best. It takes glue and still works perfectly under the plane or the rasp or in the lathe. It may be secured from any of the hardwood dealers in the large cities, Boston, particularly. It is usually sold by weight and costs from 40c to 75c a pound, according to the avarice of the dealer. The footing is cut 8 inches long and ⅜ inch square. It is slotted from one end a distance of 5⅝ inches. The making of the slot is more or less troublesome. It may be done with a hacksaw in which the blade is set at right angles with the frame. A backed saw will not reach the depth of the slot. A good hand tool for cutting the slot is made on the order of a Chinese saw, which has a rectangular shaped frame with the handle on one end and a hacksaw blade secured lengthwise in the rectangle. This permits the material to pass up through the frame without obstruction. If you have power, a five inch Disston cabinet-maker's circular saw is the best. It has no set, being thicker at the periphery than at the center. It leaves the work free from kerf and almost as smooth as if planed. If a circular saw is used the very bottom of the slot must be squared with a few strokes of a thin hacksaw blade.

The contact surfaces of the wedge and the slot are then covered with a good glue and the wedge forced into the slot, in doing which the footing is clamped in the vise up to the bottom end of the slot to avoid splitting. Before being removed from the vise clamps are applied and set firm. No fewer than three clamps for each footing should be used. More would be better. A very convenient and efficient clamp for this purpose may be made from bar steel bent into the shape of a U, provided with a $\frac{3}{16}$ inch stove bolt for a screw. The glue should be permitted to dry at least 24 hours. Any good quality of glue will do for this purpose so long as it is well dissolved and in good condition. While on the subject of glue, I wish to say that for gluing on the footings LePage's liquid glue is good. There are frequent delays and adjustments that often permit hot glue to become cold and to "cheese." The best glue I have found for this part of the work is a liquid fish glue made by the Imperial Glue Company of San Francisco. With the exception of a special glue, which will be hereafter mentioned in connection with feathering, the Imperial glue is the best I have ever found for all 'round archery tackle work.

After the clamps are removed from the footing the wings of the footing will extend beyond the sides of the shaft $\frac{3}{16}$ of an inch. These extensions should be planed off until the shaft again assumes its dimension of a straight stave $\frac{3}{8}$ of an inch square.

A grooved board, such as a piece of flooring, 36 inches long, is held in the vise with the groove uppermost in which a wooden stop near one end has been provided. The stave is laid in the groove and the four corners planed until the stave is reduced to a true octagon. The corners of the octagon are then removed in the same way and so on until the stave has been reduced to a true round. It is then further reduced with varying grades of sand paper, in doing which the arrow is given a decided spiral or rotary motion.

A power driven tool on the order of a dowel cutter is best for turning the shaft, in case the maker chooses to use a machine process.

It is best to make 18 or 24 arrows at a time. Some will turn out bad, some be ruined. The staves, although taken from the same stick, will vary in weight, often as much as 10 grains, depending upon the thickness of the year marks.

After reducing all shafts to practically the same size they are cut to the same length and the nock end of the shaft is provided with a V shaped slot for receiving the nock, which is placed there to prevent splitting by the string. The making of that slot is troublesome. It may be done by holding the rounded shaft in the vise, having provided a split block in which a hole has been bored approximately the size of the shaft, and which is used as a clamp in the vise to avoid bruising the shaft. A fine tooth hacksaw may be used. By fine tooth hacksaw I mean one made for sawing tubing, in which the teeth are double set; that is, two teeth are set to the right and then two to the left. The best one is the Globe, on sale by all first-class hardware dealers. Later I will refer to a coarse hacksaw which has the single set, such as the well-known Star. It goes without saying that a hacksaw, to be of service in working wood, should never be used on metal.

The slot for the nock may be sawed out carefully and finished with a knife-edge file. I have, however, long since abandoned that plan and instead use a circular saw specially made by myself for that purpose. It is $4\frac{1}{2}$ inches in diameter, has regular saw teeth on the periphery, on a cross-section of one-half of which shows the V shape, the saw being $\frac{3}{8}$ of an inch thick at the center and brought to a feather edge at the periphery. Long slots are cut in the saw on a tangent with a circle, the periphery of which is $\frac{3}{4}$ of an inch outside of the mandril hole. These slots are four in number and are themselves provided with teeth, the clearance being secured by grinding away the metal back of the teeth.

I realize that this is an imperfect description but I am endeavoring to describe the process without the aid of drawings and illustrations. The saw mentioned is driven at about 3,000 R.P.M. and although crude in appearance and design does the work well and almost instantly, whereas the making of the slot by hand is tedious and unsatisfactory and is often the cause of ruining partially completed shaft.

Various materials, including hard wood, horn, shell, bone, ivory, and metal, are used for nocking the arrow but the ordinary red wood-fiber, such as is extensively used in electrical work, is the best. It takes the glue well and gives the desired contrast in color, besides being exceedingly tough. The notch for the string should, however, be made across the grain. I have never known a fibre nock to split except when struck by another arrow. The nock is first reduced to the shape of a wedge 1¼ inches long and approximately the size of the V shaped slot made to receive it and be readily worked into shape by sawing with a fine tooth backed saw. A coarse hacksaw is better. The best plan, however, is to secure a strip a foot long and

⅜ of an inch thick and 1¼ inches wide, glue or screw the strip flatwise with brass screws on a strip of wood, which has been beveled on one edge at such an angle that when the wood is flat on the saw table a vertical line will pass from the corner of one edge to the opposite corner on the other edge and divide the strip of fiber in two long wedge-shaped sections. With a fine-tooth, cross-cut, circular saw, rip the strip of fiber from one end to the other. The brass screws will not injure the saw. This will produce the long, wedge-shaped strips referred to and sections may be readily cut therefrom with a coarse hack or backed saw or on the circular saw, and which sections are approximately the shape of the nock to be placed in the V shaped slot. This method saves a vast amount of work and produces nocks of uniform size. The contact surfaces of the fiber and of the slot are then covered with glue, the fiber inserted in the slot and clamped as with the footing until the glue has thoroughly dried.

 The result of the foregoing operations is a round shaft approximately 11/32 of an inch in diameter and of a length best suited to the archer, which under no circumstances should be more than 28 inches unless the archer possesses arms of unusual length and uses a bow longer than six feet. I hold that a six foot bow of the type of the English long bow, drawn more than 28 inches is abused and will not last. The shaft as so far finished will produce an arrow of approximately 5 shillings in weight, which is too heavy for a bow under 55 pounds. For weaker bows the shaft should be reduced in diameter. The rounded shaft is again placed in the grooved board and the nock end given a gradual taper with a very light cutting plane, or a wood rasp or mill-cut file, beginning 6 inches from the nock end and gradually tapering to a diameter of $9/32$ of an inch at the extreme end of the nock. The nock end is then rounded with a fine mill-cut file, or what is best a coarse emery wheel.

The notch for the string may be made in numerous ways, either with two cuts of a coarse hacksaw and then finished with a round-edged, flat file, or with a circular saw 4 inches in diameter and equal in thickness to the finished notch and rounded on the periphery to conform to the notch to the bow string. Such a saw must be kept sharp and travel at a high rate of speed, 3,000 or more. Otherwise it will tear the fiber. In cutting the V shaped slot it should be cut with the grain of the shaft. This will permit the string notch to be cut at right angles with the grain of the shaft, thereby permitting the arrow to ride the bow on the edge of the grain rather than on the flake. This is essential for two reasons. The arrow is stiffer in that direction and withstands the slap on the bow better. The other reason is that the arrow will not wear away as it would if it rides the bow on the flake. The notches in all arrows should be $\frac{3}{16}$ of an inch deep and uniform in width. They should so fit the bow string as to support the weight of the arrow when placed on the string and suspended therefrom, but the string should be made to fit the notch instead of attempting to make the notch fit the string.

The pile or arrowhead is a thimble made of steel $\frac{7}{8}$ of an inch long. They may be secured from E. I. Horsman & Company or of Mr. James Duff, manufacturer of archery tackle, or possibly from Abercrombie & Fitch of New York, who I understand have added archery tackle to their stock. I have never been able to secure a satisfactory pile. I make my own, using cylindrical sections of the required length cut from Shelby steel tubing. A pile which is a section of a true cylinder is not good; it opens a hole in the target the full size of the shaft and permits the arrow to pass entirely through the target, especially if the target be an old one. The pile should be $\frac{1}{32}$ of an inch less in diameter at the front end than at the back. This result is secured by swedging, which may be done without heating the tube. The swedge is made by boring a hole of the required size in a block of steel or brass, then reaming it with a tapered reamer. The mandrel is hardened steel of the size and shape which suggests itself from requirements. Small conical shaped points are turned from steel (cold-rolled shafting works fine); a shoulder is turned on the end of the cap so that it sets into the shell $\frac{1}{32}$ of an inch and shoulders up against the end of the shell. The cap and the shell are then soldered together. Brazing is better but unnecessary. In soldering, abandon the different acid solutions. Use any good soldering paste, that may be secured from electrical supply dealers. The caps and the shells must be carefully tinned before attempting to solder.

The pile is fitted to the end of the shaft according to the tools and conveniences at hand. The best way is with the assistance of a hollow spindle lathe, but great care should be taken to see that the pile is perfectly "stopped;" that is, the end of the shaft should come in contact with the cap of the pile and the shoulder of the shaft should meet the end of the shell, when the pile is driven home. The pile can be retained in position by glue applied to the shaft, care being taken to not use too much, otherwise the pile cannot be driven to its proper place. If it becomes necessary to remove the pile apply a flame for a short period. The gas formed by the heated glue will cause the pile to detach itself.

The shaft is again placed in the grooved board and the point of union between the footing and the pile is dressed with a mill-cut file, after which the point of the pile is dressed on the emery wheel.

At this point I wish to suggest that a tool of great convenience and utility can be easily made in the form of a wooden device carrying a handle like a plane which will clamp flat files in such position as they may be used in the same manner as a plane.

After all the shafts have been brought to the condition now referred to they are weighed upon a jeweler's balance scale until the lightest is discovered. That one should be then worked down to the desired weight and placed in the scales and all other shafts brought to equal weight. This process of reduction and weighing out is as tedious as it is important and may be performed with files, steel wool and varying grades of sand paper. The acme of finish may be secured by the use of glasspaper, which can be obtained from dealers in musical instruments and violin makers' supplies. The glasspaper leaves a finish that cannot be approached by the use of abrasive agents such as sand or emery paper, or steel wool.

Immediately after being brought to weight and before they have had opportunity to accumulate moisture the shafts should be varnished from the pile to a point within $4\frac{1}{2}$ inches of the extreme nock end. The alcohol varnishes, such as shellac are tabooed and should be avoided. They are worse than useless. Spar varnish, any of the varnishes used on bamboo fishing rods, or a good grade of rubbing varnish, which may be secured from any first-class carriage painter, may be used, but the best is what is known under the trade name of "chinamel" made by the Ohio Varnish Company. The first coat should be thinned with turpentine. The varnish used must fulfill many requirements. It must cling to a highly polished surface, must not crack under changing weather conditions, must respond to treatment with steel wool and other abrasives without gumming or balling, and at the same time must set with sufficient hardness to prevent becoming soft under the influence of frictional heat as the arrow passes into the target.

After receiving the initial coat of thin varnish the shafts are kept in a dry place for 24 hours when they again go through the weighing out process, in which they are again rubbed down with the finest grade of steel wool. No sand paper should be used; the dust will fill depressions and appear under the succeeding coats of varnish. That portion of the shaft which has not been varnished and which is called the "shaftment" is then sized with extremely thin glue and permitted to dry 6 hours. The application of the thin glue will raise the grain, which must be removed by a very light application of the fine steel wool. In applying the size, care should be taken to not cover any of the varnished portion of the shaft. If this occurs the succeeding coats of varnish will flake off. The purpose of the size will be very apparent when the operation of feathering the shaft is attempted. Without it the bare wood of the shaft will rob the feather of its glue and in addition to this the glue of the feather will not take hold of the bare wood instantly as it will if the size is used.

The fledging or feathering of an arrow, requiring as it does the securing, selection, cutting and attaching of the feather, constitutes the most difficult part of arrow making, and as frequently remarked by my good friend Challiss, is not a matter of skill but is an art.

Preëminent among feathers for a target arrow are those of the peacock, but they are almost impossible to secure. Next comes that of the domestic turkey. While the white turkey feather will not stand as much abuse as the gray, I prefer it because of its greater beauty and the fact that it can be dyed to any desired color. In attempting to dye feathers great care should be taken. If the solution is too hot it will ruin the feather. I might say that I ruin two of every three feathers I attempt to dye. Any commercial dye may be used.

What are known on the market as primary feathers or "pointers" are selected, care being taken not to select the feathers from opposite wings of the bird. They should also be selected with reference to their size and texture and if the stock on hand will permit, the portion used for fledging should come from the same part of the feather; that is, the three vanes used on an arrow should be taken from three separate feathers but from the same location for the reason that a primary feather is coarser and stiffer near its middle than at either end. Each wing on an arrow should be of precisely the same size, texture, weight and strength. A heavy vane and two light ones will have the same effect upon the flight of an arrow as would a large one and two small ones.

Feathers become seasoned and exceedingly tough and difficult to work and at a certain stage of the preparation must be rendered tractable by the application of moisture in some form referred to later. All tools used in preparing the feather must be sharp, and by this I do not mean approximately sharp. The knife that would not comfortably shave the user is not sharp enough for this purpose, and the tools must be given constant attention that they may not become dull. The feathers for a target arrow should be cut and not stripped from the bone. Using stripped feathers is but a makeshift and indicates inattention to the details so essential to final success. After the feather is selected it should be ripped lengthwise through the groove in the nether side of the bone. If the vanes are to be of the ordinary balloon shape they should be $2\frac{3}{16}$ inches long and $\frac{15}{32}$ of an inch high at the highest point. After the feather has been ripped the wings may be cut from the broad side by a die made of sheet steel, the feather being placed on a maple block and the die struck with a light hammer, care being taken not to injure the bone. Three wings may be secured from one feather and after being stamped out there will be a space between each wing, as it adheres to the bone, of about ½ inch. The die mentioned may be made from an old handsaw blade or a cabinet maker's scraper, which can be bent into shape without the application of heat. It is then sharpened on the emery wheel to a chisel edge.

The vanes as stamped are then separated by cutting the bone so as to leave ⅛ of an inch extending beyond each end of the wing. It will now be noticed that while the wing is in its final shape there is far too much bone attached to it and this excess of bone for convenience is described as follows: That portion which lies in the same plane with the cane is "A;" that portion which lies in a plane at right angles to that of the vane is "B." The surplus at "B" is removed by being held in a clamp and cut with the blade of a safety razor. The clamp is in the form of an ordinary butt hinge having three leaves and is made preferably of aluminum to avoid dulling the knife. The two outside leaves are of strong metal, reinforced with wood to prevent bending or giving under the strain. The middle leaf is made of very thin aluminum or brass about 36 gauge. The feather as stamped is placed in the clamp with the vane firmly held between the middle leaf and one of the outer leaves of the clamp. The safety razor blade is then inserted between the middle leaf and the other outside leaf of the clamp in such manner that the middle leaf lies between the blade and the vane of the feather. A single stroke of the blade suffices to remove the surplus bone at "B" and the vane of the feather is protected, by the intervening middle leaf, from damage during the operation. The result is that the surplus bone left at "B" will be equal to the thickness of the middle leaf in the hinged clamp. There is still far too much bone at "A," the removal of which gives no little trouble. The following plan is the result of many experiments both in method and with mechanical devices.

As before stated, the feather becomes seasoned and tough and at this stage it is necessary to soften the bone by the application of moisture. In fact, that may be done before removing the surplus at "B" but it is not so essential. A shallow pan is so arranged over the gas flame that water placed therein will be slowly evaporated. The pan has a cover of galvanized wire screen. A piece of heavy cloth (an old bath towel is good) is wrung out of hot water and then laid on top of the screen in such manner that the vanes as stamped out may be arranged on top of the cloth and then covered with a fold of the same cloth. The heat and moisture from the cloth, to which is added the heat and vapor from the evaporating water, will in 10 or 15 minutes render the feathers soft and pliable. As needed, they are removed from the steam bath, care being taken to keep those not in use covered with the extra fold of the cloth. One vane is removed from the steam bath and laid upon a smooth, soft pine board, crosswise of the grain of the board. Lack of attention to this apparently small detail will absolutely baffle any attempt to cut the bone of the feather "A," which is the desideratum. The vane is held on the pine block with a straight edge 4 inches long, $\frac{3}{8}$ of an inch thick and $1\frac{1}{4}$ inches wide, brought to a beveled edge in the form of an ordinary ruler. The sole purpose of the straight edge is for the purpose of holding the vane firmly in position while being cut. The knife does not touch the straight edge during the process of cutting. The straight edge is placed on the vane and the straight line of the bone left in removing the surplus at "B" is pressed firmly and accurately against the straight edge and the surplus bone at "A" is removed by a single stroke of the knife guided only by the eye. The best knife for this purpose is made from an old-fashioned razor blade $5/8$ of an inch wide, the point of which has been left at right angles and not rounded and to which blade has been affixed securely and firmly a wooden handle according to the individual desire of the fletcher. In operation, the point of the blade passes through the bone and into the soft pine board and assists in guiding the knife. It will therefore be readily seen that if the cut were made with the grain of the pine board the knife would follow the grain of the wood and be deflected. It is possible to make this last and most important cut by several successive strokes of the knife but the result is never so satisfactory. It should be done at a single stroke. Should the result be other than a perfectly true line the following makeshift may be resorted to. Replace the vane in the hinge clamp, bring the surface of the bone at "A" to a true line by filing it with a file made by gluing a strip of sharp sand paper (oo grade) on a stick 8 or 9 inches long and ⅜ of an inch square. I have heard of arrow makers who instead of cutting their feathers remove the surplus bone by holding the vane in a clamp and planing off the surplus with a tiny violin maker's plane. I have tried it without the slightest degree of success. After the final cut the vane is restored to the vapor bath where it remains until the balance of the vanes receive the finishing cut.

There are numerous methods of gluing the vane to the shaft. One is by temporarily wrapping them on with thread. This is the poorest possible method and unworkmanlike. Another way is by placing the vane between the leaves of a clamp such as would be formed by an ordinary butt hinge and pressing the glue-covered surface of the bone against the shaft. This requires too much manipulation, is uncertain in adhesive results and clumsy to a degree. I have a mechanical device made by myself which will feather any arrow perfectly but any mechanical device requires so many different manipulations that it appeals only to those who lack the skill required to do the work properly without mechanical aids. The best plan for the skilled workman is to simply pick up the feather, apply glue to the contact surface of the bone, and stick it in position, but the knack only comes with long, patient practice and is fully as difficult as is the foregoing statement simple. For the benefit of advanced arrow makers, I beg to state, however, that it is the best way to feather arrows, and from every viewpoint it is the best. It requires no preparatory manipulation of the feather, the result is satisfying, and operation brief. I might say that in feathering my first arrows I resorted to the plan of wrapping them on with thread which held them in position while the glue dried. It required 2 hours to feather a single arrow and the result was anything but satisfactory. Years afterward on one occasion, by following the plan of simply "sticking them on," I feathered an even dozen arrows in thirteen minutes.

For the purpose of this article and of those for whose benefit it is written, I assert the following method of attaching the feathers to the shaft to be the best. If instructions have been followed to date the bone of the wing will extend at right angles from the vane about $\frac{1}{10}$ of an inch and the thickness of the bone at the point of contact with the shaft described as "A," will be about the same. The bone will extend beyond each end of the vane ⅛ of an inch. A supply of bead-headed steel pins about 1¼ inches in length should be secured. One pin is passed through the extension of the bone at the nock end of the vane, the point of the pin barely passing through the bone. Another pin is passed $\tfrac{1}{16}$ of an inch through the extension of bone on the opposite or pile end of the vane, but instead of being at right angles with the axis of the bone as is the first pin, it is placed at an angle of about 45 degrees, slanting toward the nock end of the vane. The glue is then applied in small quantities to the surface of the bone which will rest upon the shaft, in doing which a small sliver of wood serves the purpose better than a brush. The cock feather, being the one which is placed at right angles with the string notch, is the first to be applied and so placed that the distance between the extreme nock end of the shaft and the end of the vane is 1⅛ inches. While held in that position pin number 1 is pressed home. This will necessitate pressing the pin into the fibre nock, but that may be readily done. Pin number 2, which has been hanging in the loose end of the bone, is than grasped, the feather drawn taut and the point of pin number 2, which protrudes through the bone $\frac{1}{16}$ of an inch, is pressed slightly into the shaft, being careful still to retain the 45 degree angle. When the footing has been thus secured, pin number 2 is brought to a position at right angles with the axis of the shaft and pressed home. It will be noted that this operation secures a leverage which stretches the bone of the feather tight against the shaft and forces out any surplus glue. If the work is carefully performed there will be no surplus glue. The other two feathers are placed on the shaft in the same manner, being careful to accurately divide the total circumference of the shaft into three equal parts. This division may be made with the aid of instruments, laying off the different points of contact, but that is unnecessary labor. Practice will enable the workman to space those distances instantly by the eye and so accurately that they will not vary the distance of one of the holes made by the pin point. One hour is sufficient time to permit the drying of the

Notes on Arrow Making

glue, after which the pins are removed, the bone extension at the nock end is cut square, and the bone extension at the other end is trimmed to a feather edge with the feather knife.

The very best glue used for attaching the feathers is made of equal parts of the best commercial glue and Russian isinglass. Do not confuse isinglass with mica. The isinglass, after being cut with shears into small bits, is soaked for two days in sufficient water to cover it, together with the commercial glue, to which should be added brandy, quantity sufficient. It is then brought to a boil in an ordinary glue pot in a water bath. Brandy must be added from time to time as needed and small quantities of the glue cooked up as needed. Notwithstanding the use of brandy the glue ferments within a few days and gives off a very offensive odor. The Russian isinglass costs from 40c to 60c an ounce and may be secured from the large drug houses. It is, however, not expensive because of the great bulk in a given weight.

The entire arrow is next varnished from nock to pile with thin varnish, being careful to lay the varnish well over the glue joint formed by the union of the feather and shaft but keep it from coming into contact with the vane of the feather. If it does, the varnish will creep up the vanes, make them stiff and mar the looks. After this coat of varnish has thoroughly dried it is again cut down with the fine steel wool; the uniform weight of the arrows being maintained. The shaftment, being the space between a point $\frac{15}{16}$ of an inch from the extreme nock end to a point $4\frac{3}{4}$ inches from the extreme nock end is then painted any desired color, in doing which the paint is laid up, on and over the bone of the feather but not permitted to touch the vane. This is best done with a small round brush in which the bristles are about a half inch long, ending in a point. The crest is then painted on, using one wide band and several narrow ones or two or more wide ones, lined with a color different from any used in the crest. The lining is best done in a lathe but can be accomplished by laying the arrow in a notch cut in the work bench and twirling it with one hand while applying the paint lines with the other. For lining, I find a very fine pointed brush the easiest to handle. The band nearest the nock end is about $\frac{3}{16}$

of an inch wide, leaving the final ¾ inch of the nock end bare of paint. The appearance is, however, fully preserved by the contrast between the wood of the shaft and the red fiber nock.

After the paint has dried the entire arrow is again varnished with a coat of varnish that has not been thinned, and after that has dried the arrow is again rubbed down with the fine steel wool and polished with a dry woolen cloth.

Hunting arrows are made of hickory $11/32$ of an inch in diameter and 28 inches long. It is not necessary to foot them nor to reinforce the string notch with a nock. The feathers are stripped from the bone instead of being cut. Unless properly stripped, small particles of pith will adhere to the skin of bone that remains attached to the vane. To avoid this, take the feather just as it leaves the bird, grasp it at the outer or vane end with thumb and finger of left hand, holding the feather in a vertical position. With the thumb and finger of the right hand tear the vane loose from the bone near the vane end and immediately turn the torn part downward making and maintaining a sharp angle between the torn part of the vane and the bone of the feather, then pull downward; the vane will strip off the entire length of the feather and will come away clean. If too much of the bone-skin comes off with the vane, it may be trimmed with the shears. The vanes of a hunting arrow are 4 inches long and ⅞ of an inch high. The big softer feathers of the wing yield better vanes than do the primary or pointers. The vanes are attached in like manner as to a target arrow but if placed with a slight twist or spiral the flight of the arrow will probably be improved 50 per cent. Indeed I feather all my target arrows with the same twist or spiral suggested for hunting arrows. If the pile end of the vane is placed 3/32 of an inch out of line with the axis of the shaft there will be ample twist to the vane. In fledging an arrow with spiral or twist wings, care must be taken to so place them that the pressure of the air on the vanes while in flight will come against what would be the nether side of the feather when in the wing of the bird, as the vane of a feather is very stiff in that direction while in the other it is limber.

Hunting arrows are headed according to

the use intended. Babbitt headed blunt arrows are used in shooting at birds and small game in trees and sharp steel bladed ones for large game and game on the ground. The weight of hunting arrows should be as nearly uniform as practicable, but nothing like the great care in this respect is required as in the target arrow. They should be painted between the feathers and varnished to exclude moisture from shaft and vane. White feathers and a red shaftment have saved from oblivion many an honest shaft.

CHAPTER XXIV

THE COMPOSITE BOW

By Samuel G. McMeen

FOR long distance shooting, irrespective of the hitting of a mark, the bow having most to its credit is that made and used by the Turks. Three features distinguish such a bow from the English longbow: that it is shorter, that it is strongly reflexed, (being in this regard the prototype of the Cupid's bow) and that it is composite, being made of wood, horn and sinew or an equivalent of the latter.

Elsewhere in this book are told the details of the shooting of these bows. Mahmoud Effendi, a Turk, in 1795 shot a Turkish arrow 482 yards from a Turkish composite bow. Ingo Simon, an Englishman, in 1913, at Le Toquet, France, shot an arrow 459 yards, 8 inches from a composite Turkish bow. No English longbow has approached these distances. The difference is in the bow and not in any secret of its use.

The bow used by Ingo Simon is said to have been made in 1835, and that the secret of the making has been lost. It is not known that a successful composite, reflexed, flight-shooting bow ever was made by a man of the Anglo-Saxon race before the summer of 1917.

In that year, Dr. Saxton T. Pope, a surgeon of San Francisco, made such a weapon, and the editors are indebted to him for the details on which the following description is based.

The materials are of vegetable and animal origin; that is, wood, horn, rawhide and catgut. These materials are assembled so that all of them are present throughout the length of the bow. The central "backbone" is of white hickory; it is slightly oval in cross-section; length, fifty-three inches, width, one and a half inches and thickness five-sixteenths inch. The horn portion is built up of strips, and forms the belly of the bow. The hickory is backed by the rawhide and catgut, and the whole is enclosed in more rawhide.

These details will appear more clearly by following the steps taken by Dr. Pope in the actual making of the bow.

From the longest cow-horns obtainable, he cut strips half an inch wide, a quarter of an inch thick, and as long as possible, he mitred across the half-inch dimension, and fitted the strips together in three parallel columns on the hickory base. Care was taken to "break joints" in this arrangement. The horn strips were softened in hot water at the time of application to the base. Organ glue was used for the attachment.

At this point, the ends of the bow were given the reflex; that is, the ends of the wood and horn bend backward, the horn being on the convex side. Glue applied plentifully, heavy binding with strong twine, supplemented by many clamps.

After a week's drying, the clamps and twine were removed and the horn rasped into shape, giving it a general thickness of a quarter of an inch, but thickest in the mid-limbs. Then the following sequence: a backing of thin rawhide attached by liquid glue; drying; a layer of one hundred strands of No. 3 catgut laid side by side on the rawhide in liquid glue; these bound on by a gauze bandage; drying; removal of bandage; scraping; shaping; another layer of rawhide over the parallel strands of catgut.

After still more drying, the bow now was given horn nocks and these provided with lateral notches to keep the string from slipping off of the strongly bent extremities when the bow should be fully drawn.

More drying; filing the horn side to symmetrical and supposedly proper proportions; binding again with cord and testing the curve and weight; to make these adjustments all the reduction was done upon the horn; horn ears were set on the belly of the bow three inches from the tips.

All now was covered with rawhide. This was softened in warm water and attached by organ glue; bandaged; dried, unbandaged; scraped; sand papered; wrappings of linen thread at a few places symmetrically chosen in each limb (to safeguard against the parts separating); a handle of leather was applied, a finish of shellac and oil; at this point the bow was well dried.

The string is of Pagenstecher thread, a material used by surgeons, laid up with double loops after the manner of Maxson as elsewhere described in this book, served not only at the nocking point but at the points where the string engages the ears mentioned as being placed three inches from the tips. The purpose of these ears is not, as some authors seem to think, to assist in "bracing" the bow, but to afford for the string a fulcrum or resting spot to insure a clear release. Otherwise the string would buzz on the reversed outer limb. In other words, the formation is such as to shorten the chord of the arc abruptly, giving a quick vibration to the string.

At the time of this writing this first Anglo-Saxon-built composite flight-shooting Turkish-type bow has not seasoned to a point to give final account of its powers. In preliminary trials, however, it has demonstrated great driving ability. One of its earliest shots in trial was but ten yards short of the present American flight-shot record. What it yet shall do will be interesting to be seen. The details will appear in the succeeding editions of this book.

CHAPTER XXV

Glossary

By Dr. Robert P. Elmer

Allowance. Change in aim to compensate for windage.

Arbalist. A crossbow.

Armguard. A piece of leather or other stiff material worn on the left forearm to protect it from injury by the bowstring. Also called *Bracer*.

Arrow horn. A V-shaped piece of horn, fibre or similar material inserted in the posterior end of an arrow and containing the nock. Modern arrows are sometimes fitted with an aluminum ferrule to which the name may probably be extended. (See *Nock 3*.)

Arrow plate. A thin piece of hard material set in the bow, where it is crossed by the arrow, to prevent wear.

Arrowsmith. A fletcher.

Arrow stave. A slender rod of wood ready for further shaping to form a stele.

Artillery. A word originally meaning bows and arrows.

Archer's rod. A measure of 7½ yards.

Ascham (aś-kam). 1. A tall, narrow cabinet for bows, arrows and other tackle.
2. A portable case for bows and arrows.

Back. 1. The flat side of a bow.
2. To glue a strip of wood or other elastic material to the back of the self bow.

Backed bow. A bow whose back and belly are of different strips of wood glued together. Rawhide or other animal tissue is sometimes used for backing.

Backing. Material from which the back of a backed bow is made.

Balloon feather. A vane of parabolic outline.

Barrelled arrow. An arrow that is larger in the middle than at the ends.

Bass. The straw back of a target.

Belly. The round side of a bow.

Bend. 1. To string a bow, not to draw it.
2. The space between the bent bow and its string.

Bobtailed arrow. An arrow whose shaft is a cone with the base at the pile.

Bolt. A short, thick arrow used in a crossbow.

Bow-arm. The arm that supports the bow.

Bow-hand. The hand that holds the bow.

Bowman. An archer.

Bow stave. See *Stave*.

Bowyer. A maker of bows.

Brace. To bend a bow.

Bracer. An armguard.

Butt. An artificial embankment of sod or earth against which a target or prick is placed.

Cast. 1. The coefficients of resilience of a bow.
2. The distance a given bow can shoot.
3. A tilt in the back of a bow out of the perpendicular to the plane passing through the string and the longitudinal center of the bow.
4. Any lateral warping of a bow.

Chested arrow. An arrow whose shaft is a cone with the base at the nock.

Chrysal (kriś–al). A transverse fault in the belly of a bow caused by compression. Also called *Pinch*.

Cloth yard. A measure of probably 27 inches.

Clout. 1. A small cloth or other white object placed on the ground as a mark in long distance shooting. The modern clout is a straw backed, white faced target with a black spot in the center. It is 30 inches in diameter and is set on the ground at an angle of 60 degrees. 2. A hit in the clout.

Cock feather. The vane that stands at right angles to the nock.

Come. A bow is said to *come* when it bends too much in one place.

Composite bow. A bow made of three layers of materials, usually sinew back, wood center and horn belly.

Crest. Colored rings painted about the shaft of an arrow above the feathers, for identification.

Crossbow. A missive weapon formed by a bow fixed athwart a stock in which there is a groove or barrel to direct the missile, a notch or catch to hold the string when the bow is bent, and a trigger to release it. (Century Dictionary.)

Curl. A sudden turn in the grain of the wood of a bow.

Cut the gold. An expression signifying the apparent dropping across the gold of an arrow which falls short.

Cut the mark. Similar to *Cut the gold* but used for any object aimed at, as in rovers or hunting.

Damp sap. A bluish line between the heart and sap-wood in yew.

Dead loose. A sluggish release.

Dead shaft. An arrow of dull, heavy flight.

Direction. Same as *Line of aim*.

Direct vision. The formation of the sight image at the *macula lutea*. Whatever is seen most clearly is in direct vision.

Double round. Two identical rounds shot in succession and the results added.

Down wind. A wind blowing from the archer to the target.

Draw. 1. To pull the bowstring back as in shooting.
2. The distance the string is pulled.

Draw a feather. To strip the web from the shaft of a feather.

Drawing arm. The arm that draws the string. Also called *Shaft arm*.

Drawing fingers. The first three fingers of the drawing hand.

Drawing hand. The hand of the drawing arm. The right hand in right handed archers and the left in left handed. Also called *Shaft hand*.

Draw through a bow. To draw so far that the pile passes the belly.

Drift. Same as *Windage*.

Elevation. The relative height of the pile to the nock in aiming an arrow.

End. 1. In England, three arrows shot consecutively.
2. In America, six arrows shot consecutively or in pairs (threes).
3. The position of a mark.

Eye. The upper loop of a string.

Fast. An exclamation used as a warning of danger, as is "Fore" in golf.

Feather. 1. A vane.
2. A layer f the grain in yew.
3. The feathered end or string end of an arrow. (Century Dictionary.)

4. To fit with a feather or feathers, as an arrow. (Century Dictionary.)

Feather in. To imbed an arrow in its mark as far as the feathers.

Finger tip. A leather thimble to protect a drawing finger.

Fish. The joint of the two limbs of a yew bow.

Fish tail. A staggering arrow.

Fistmele. A measure of 6 inches. It is believed by many to be the correct distance between the string and the bent bow and is usually found by placing the fist upright upon the inside of the bow handle and raising the thumb.

Fletch. To feather an arrow. (Century Dictionary.)

Fletcher. 1. A maker of arrows.
2. One who feathers arrows.
3. A maker of bows and arrows. (Century Dictionary.)
Also called Arrowsmith.

Flight arrow. A light arrow for flight shooting.

Flight shot. A shot for great distance without regard to aim.

Follow the string. An expression denoting the permanent set or curve that a bow takes on from being bent and drawn.

Footed arrow. An arrow whose anterior portion is formed of a piece of hard wood spliced to the main part of the shaft.

Foot. A piece of hard wood spliced on the anterior end of a shaft and forming an integral part of it. Also called pileing and footing.

Fret. A fault in the wood of a bow, such as a chrysal or corroded spot.

Grip. 1. The handle of a bow.
2. The manner of grasping a bow.

Gone. An arrow is gone when it flies above the target.

Handle. The part of a bow that is grasped in the hand.

Hard handled bow. A bow which does not bend at the grip.

Head. Same as *pile*.

He! He! The time honored word of call used by archers in hailing each other from a distance. (Dr. Weston.)

Hen feathers. The two vanes that lie at an angle of 30 degrees to the nock.

High feathered. Having long, deep feathers.

Hit. 1. To strike a mark with an arrow.
2. The striking of a mark with an arrow. If the mark be a target the arrow must remain in it, neither rebounding nor passing through.

Holding. Keeping an arrow fully drawn for a moment before it is loosed.

Home. An arrow is *home* when fully drawn.

Horn. A bow tip.

Horn spoon. 1. A hit in the petticoat.
2. The petticoat.

Hoyle-shooting. Same as roving.

Indirect vision. Formation of the sight image at some part of the retina other than the *macula lutea.* (Century Dictionary.)

In game. In good shooting cue.

Keeping a length. Shooting with consistently correct elevation at a given distance.

Keeping compass. Same as *keeping a length.*

Kick. The jar to the hand caused by a discharging bow, due to faulty construction of the weapon.

Lapping. A wrapping of thread around a bow to strengthen it or around a string to protect it from abrasion. Also called *Serving, Whipping* and *Wrapping.*

Lay the body in the bow. An old English expression which suggests that drawing should be done with the shoulders as well as the arms.

Length. A distance to be shot.

Let fly. To release an arrow.

Line of aim. The vertical plane of an imaginary line from the archer's eye to the centre of the target. Also called *Direction.*

Longbow. The name commonly given to the bow drawn by hand and discharging a long feathered arrow, as distinguished from crossbows of all kinds, especially to bows having a length of five feet or over, as the bow of war and of the chase of the middle ages of Europe, those of some savage tribes, those of Japan, etc. (Century Dictionary.)

Loose. 1. To release the string when fully drawn.

2. The manner of releasing the string when drawn.

Low feathered. Having short shallow feathers.

Mark. 1. Anything that is shot at.
2. To signal results in clout shooting.

Marker. A man who stands near a clout to signal to the archers the results of their shots.

Nock. 1. The groove for the string in the tip of a bow.
2. The slot in the end of an arrow.
3. The piece of hard material at the end of an arrow which contains the slot for the string. Also called *Arrow horn.*
4. The act of slipping the loop of the string into a nock.
5. The act of fitting an arrow to the string.

Nocking point. The exact place on the string where an arrow should be nocked, often marked with thread or ink.

Noose. The loop at the lower end of the string.

Overbowed. Using a bow beyond one's strength.

Overstrung. Said of a bow whose string is too short.

Pair. In archery three arrows, not two, are called a pair.

Paper game. Shooting at a small bit of paper, often about an inch in diameter, which is pinned to a butt.

Penny. A measure of weight for arrows equal to $7\frac{1}{4}$ grains.

Petticoat. 1. A hit in the petticoat.
2. The rim of the target outside of the white ring. It has no value. Also called *Horn Spoon* and *Spoon*.

Piecing. Same as *Foot*.

Pile. A ferrule covering the anterior end of an arrow. It may be sharp or blunt and made of any hard substance. Also called *Head*, *Tip* and *Point*.

Pin. A tiny knot in yew wood, appearing on the surface as a black spot.

Pinch. Same as *Chrysal*.

Play in the hand. Said of a bow which bends at the grip.

Point. 1. Same as *Pile*.
2. A unit of scoring.
3. A unit of a specified total, based on the highest score or greatest number of hits at given distances.

Point blank. 1. Aim taken at a distance where the point of aim and centre of the target coincide.
2. Aim taken at a distance so short that the arrow flies in a trajectory that is practically flat.
Point of aim. An object so situated that if the tip of a fully drawn arrow be brought into the imaginary line between it and the eye, that arrow, when loosed, if all other factors be perfect, will hit the centre of the target.
Popinjay. A small wooden bird on the top of a pole, used as a mark.
Prick. A small mark on a butt.
Prick shooting. Shooting at a prick.
Prince's lengths. The three distances of the York round.
Quartering wind. A wind blowing obliquely across the range.
Quiver. 1. A portable receptacle for arrows, carried attached to the person by a strap or hook.
2. The coming to rest of an arrow in what it hits. For example, "The arrow quivered in a tree," means that it stopped there, not that it trembled.

Range. 1. A shooting ground.
2. A length or distance to be shot.

Reflexed bow. A bow in which a concave, obtuse angle is formed by the backs of the two limbs when unstrung.

Release. Same as *loose*.

Round. A prescribed number of shots at prescribed distances. There are ten recognized rounds, which are named and constituted as follows:

1. American Round	30 arrows at	60 yards
	30 " "	50 "
	30 " "	40 "
2. Columbia Round	24 " "	50 "
	24 " "	40 "
	24 " "	30 "
3. Hereford Round	48 " "	80 "
	24 " "	60 "
4. National Round	48 " "	60 "
	24 " "	50 "
5. Potomac Round	24 " "	80 "
	24 " "	70 "
	24 " "	60 "
6. St. George's Round	36 " "	100 "
	36 " "	80 "
	36 " "	60 "
7. St. Leonard's Round	36 " "	80 "
	39 " "	60 "
(Originally it was	75 " "	60 "
8. Team Round, Men	96 " "	60 "
9. Team Round, Women	96 " "	50 "
10. York Round	72 " "	100 "
	48 " "	80 "
	24 " "	60 "

Nos. 5, 6 and 7 of the above are practically obsolete.

Glossary

Rovers. An archery pastime which consists in shooting at one mark after another, each mark being at a distance from the last. It may be played over a prescribed course in a manner similar to golf or the marks may be selected at random.

Rover's mark. A mark shot at in rovers.

Roving. Playing rovers, not simply roaming.

Self arrow. An arrow made of a single piece of wood, not footed.

Self bow. A bow each limb of which is made of a single, unbacked piece of wood. It may or may not be fished at the grip.

Serving. Same as *Lapping*.

Set the shaft in the bow. To draw it so far that the tip catches on the belly.

Shaft. 1. The wooden part of an arrow. Also called *Stele*.
2. An arrow.

Shaft arm. The drawing arm.

Shaft hand. The drawing hand.

Shaftment. The part of an arrow where the feathers are.

Shake. A longitudinal crack in wood.

Sharp loose. A quick release.

Sheaf of arrows. Twenty-four arrows in a case. Used in military archery.

Shilling. A measure of weight for arrows, of 87¼ grains.

Shooting glove. 1. In Scotland a large glove for the drawing hand with the first three fingers reinforced on the palmar surface and a pocket in the back for extra strings.
2. Any glove for the drawing hand, usually having the tips of the drawing fingers reinforced.

Shoot in a bow. The old English way of saying, "Shoot a bow."

Side wind. A wind blowing at right angles to the line of aim.

Sink a bow. To reduce its weight.

Slash. To loose in a quick, plucking manner.

Snake. 1. An arrow buried in the grass, lying flat to the ground.
2. For an arrow to bury itself in the grass.

Spell. A rising of the ends of the grain in the wood of a bow.

Splinter. A small, flat sliver of wood split from the back of a bow but still attached at one end.

Spoon. Same as *Horn spoon* and *Petticoat*.

Spine. The degree of stiffness of an arrow.

Stagger. To wobble. Said of an arrow in flight. Also called *Wag*.

Standard yard. A measure of 36 inches.

Stele. The wooden part of an arrow.

Stopping. The solid part of a pile.

Sweet. Said of a bow which does not kick.

Stave or Bowstave. A long, slender piece of wood of which a bow may be made.

Tab. A flat piece of leather large enough to cover the palmar surface of the drawing fingers and used to prevent abrasion of the skin. It is kept in place by sticking the first and third fingers through hole. Between the first and second fingers is a slot for the nock of the arrow.

Tackle. All the equipment of an archer.

Tassel. A tassel, usually made of green worsted, suspended from the archer's belt to wipe his arrows with.

Tiller. A stick with notches in the side and ends, used to hold a bow drawn while it is being made or repaired. One end is placed against the inside of the handle and the string is caught in a notch at the desired distance.

Tillering. The act of using a tiller, including the scraping of the bow.

Tip. 1. A pile.
2. A reinforcement of leather on the fingers of a shooting glove.
3. To apply such reinforcements.
4. A thimble, or similar device of leather or other material, for each of the shooting fingers.
5. A bow horn.

Toxophilite. A student of archery; one who practices archery; one who studies the history and archeology of archery. (Century Dictionary.)

Toxophilitic. Relating or pertaining to archery or to the study of archery.

Trajectory. The path of an arrow in the air.

Turtle-back shooting. Shooting high in the air so that the arrow, on returning, may hit a target laid flat on the ground. So called because South American Indians are said to shoot turtles in that way.

Underbowed. Using a bow beneath one's strength.

Glossary

Underhand shooting. Shooting with the bow held so that the point of aim is seen under the bow hand.

Understrung. Said of a bow whose string is too long.

Up wind. A wind blowing from the target to the archer.

Vane. A piece of feather tied or glued to the shaft near the nock to direct the flight of an arrow. Three are usually placed on each arrow.

Wag. Same as *Stagger*.

Weight. 1. The avoirdupois weight of an arrow expressed in grains or in shillings and pence.
2. The force required to draw a bow the length of its arrow. For example, a man's bow weighing 46 pounds is one whose string will be drawn 28 inches from the back of the handle by a 46 pound stress.

Weight in hand. The avoirdupois weight of a bow.

Wen. An excrescence in the wood of a bow.

Whale backed bow. A bow whose belly is almost wedge shaped. (Duff.)

Whipping. Same as *Lapping*.

Wide. An arrow is *wide* when it flies to one side or the other of the target.

Windage. 1. The influence of the wind in deflecting an arrow.
2. The extent of such deflection.
Also called *Drift*.

Wrapping. Same as *Lapping*.

James Duff

Bowyer and Fletcher

130 Zabriskie Street
JERSEY CITY, New Jersey

Bows, Arrows and Accessories
made especially to order

Material and Workmanship Guaranteed

H. H. McChesney

Bowyer and Fletcher

2414 Portland Avenue
MINNEAPOLIS, Minnesota

Bows, Arrows and Accessories
made especially to order

Material and Workmanship Guaranteed

This Book

AMERICAN ARCHERY

is an official publication of the
*National Archery Association of the
United States*

It is for sale by the Association

Price $2.50 a copy

Address orders to the
Publication Committee
National Archery Association
1003 Huntington Bank Building
COLUMBUS, OHIO, U. S. A.

Index

A

Aiming, 25.
Aim, point of, 27.
Amaranth, 251.
American round, 51.
Antient Scorton arrow, 146, 147.
Archers' Manual, 9.
Archers, Royal Company of, 152.
Archery, American, Hisotory of, 7.
    club, to form, 63.
    correct, study of, 21.
    Association, Chicago, 11.
    Association, National, 47.
    Association, Eastern, 103.
    Belgian, 178.
    French, 178.
    The Witchery of, 11.
Arrow, Antient Scorton, 146, 147.
    Duff, 59.
    feathers, 264.
    Maid Marian, 61, 102.
    making, 247.
    nocks, 34.
    pile, 259.
Arrowhead, 176.
Arrows, 33.
    feathering, 265.
    hunting, 277.
    Reddendo, 152.
    sizing, 264.
    weights of, 35.
    woods for, 250, 251.
Artillery, 33.
Ascham, Roger, 21.

B

Backed bow, 215, 237.
Beefwood, 251.
Beginners, hints to, 40.
Belgian Archery, 178.
Black locust wood, 197.
Bow, backed, 215, 237.
    composite, 280.
    for flight shooting, 161.
    Persian, 161.
    rawhide backed, 240.
    selecting, 37.
    Turkish, 161, 163.
    weight of, 37.
Bowmaking, 192, 220.
Bowstring, 244.
Bracer, 37.
Bugle, Pearsall, 59.

C

Chicago Archery Association, 11.
Club, Archery, to form, 63.
Columbia round, 51.
Composite bows, 161.
Constitution of the N. A. A., 47.
Cup, Chicago, 100.
    Clan McLeod, 59, 97, 101.
    Jiles, 59, 98, 99, 100.
    Ovington, 59, 101.
    Peacock, 61, 102.
    Weston, 62, 101.

D

Dallin Medal, 3.
Deming, Frederick, 173.
Drawing, 24.

E.

Eastern Archery Association, 103.
Ebony, 251.
Elmer wooden spoon, 59, 101.
Equipment, 33.

F

Feather glue, 275.
Feathers, cutting, 266.
    dyeing, 264.
    for arrows, 34, 264.
Feats of skill, 114.
Fibre, wood, for arrow nocks, 256.
Finger, The "Shirking First," 30.
    tips, 37.
Fish joint, 212, 226.
Flight arrows, 164.
    shooting, 160.
Ford, Horace A., 69.
French Archery, 178.

G

Game shooting, 134, 140, 141, 149, 150.
Glass ball shooting, 149, 151.
Glossary of terms, 285.
Glove, shooting, 37, 45.
Glue for feathers, 275.
    spirit, 275.
Grip, 24.

H

Hiawatha's feat, 141.
Hints to beginners, 40.
Holding, 29.
Hosking, A. N., 3.

I

Indian Boy trophy, 4, 61, 100, 101, 102.
Isinglass, Russian, 275.
Ishi, 144.

L

Lancewood, 183.
Le Coq, 181.
Lemonwood, 183.
Loose, primary, 139.
    tertiary, 134.
Loosing, 30.

M

Mahmoud Effendi, 161, 280.
Mahogany, 251.
Medal, Beach, 61.
    Christian Science Monitor, 99, 102.
    Dallin, 4, 61, 100, 101, 102.
    Duff, 101.
    Maurice Thompson, 58, 100.
    Potomac, 58, 100.
    Sidway, 61.
    Spalding, 58, 61, 100.
Mulberry wood, 197.

N

National Archery Association of the United States, 47.
National round, 51.
Nocking, 23.
Nocks, arrow, 34.

O

Osage Orange wood, 183.

P

Pausing, 31.
Peale, Titian Ramsay, 8.
Persian bows, 161.

Pile, arrow, 259.
Point of aim, 27, 42, 171.
Points, scoring by, 156.
Pope, Dr. Saxton T., composite bow, 280.
    "Seven-arrows-in-the-air", 141.
Popinjay, 180.

Q

Quiver, 38.

R

Rawhide backing, 35, 240.
Reddendo arrows, 152.
Robin Hood, 7.
Rosewood, 251.
Rounds, all, defined, 51.
Royal Company of Archers, 152.
Russian isinglass, 275.

S

Scores, American, 67, 78, 85.
    English, 69.
Scorton arrow, 146, 147.
"Seven-arrows-in-the-air", 141.
Shilling, unit of weight, 35.
Simon, Ingo, 161, 280.
Sizing arrows, 264.
Snakewood, 251.
Spirit glue, 275.
Spoon, Elmer wooden, 59, 101.
Stand, target, 39.

Standing, 22.
Strings, 38.

T

Target, 39, 52.
    stand, 39.
Terms, Glossary of, 285.
Thompson, Maurice, 10, 149, 151.
Thompson, Will H., 10.
Toxophilus, Ascham's, 21.
Trophy, Jessop, 61.
    Weston, 62, 101.
Turkish bows, 161, 163, 280.

U

United Bowman of Philadelphia, 8.

V

Vulcanized fiber, for arrow nocks, 256.

W

Washaba wood, 183.
Weight of bows, 37.
Witchery of Archery, The, 11.
Wood fiber, for arrow nocks, 256.
Woods for arrows, 250, 251.
    for bows, 183.

Y

Yew, 183, 195, 220.
York round, 51.

www.ingramcontent.com/pod-product-compliance
Lightning Source LLC
Chambersburg PA
CBHW032001220426
43664CB00005B/96